Contents

Unit 1 Making friends

Getting to know you

1 About you 1

Grammar and vocabulary

A Complete the chart with the words in the box.

class	fun	movies	only child	TV
college	major	✓ neighborhood	parents	

Home and family	School	Free time
neighborhood		

B Answer the questions with your own information. Use short answers.

1. Are you an only child? _Yes, I am._ **or** _No, I'm not._
2. Is your neighborhood quiet? _____
3. Do you live with your parents? _____
4. Do you have a big TV? _____
5. Do you and your friends go to college? _____
6. Are you a French major? _____
7. Does your best friend like action movies? _____
8. Is your English class fun? _____

2 You and me

Grammar Complete the conversation with the verb *be*. Use contractions where possible.

Koji Hi. I'_m_ Koji.

Isabel Hi. I _____ Isabel. Where _____ you from, Koji?

Koji I _____ from Japan. How about you?

Isabel Mexico, from Monterrey.

Koji Oh, my friends Manuel and Rosa _____ from Mexico, too.

Isabel Really? _____ your friends here now?

Koji No, they _____ not. Uh, I guess they _____ late.

Isabel _____ the teacher here?

Koji Yes, she _____ . She _____ over there.

Isabel She looks nice. What _____ her name?

Koji I think it _____ Ms. Barnes.

TOUCHSTONE

SUSAN RIVERS
GEORGIANA FARNOAGA

WITHDRAWN

WORKBOOK

CAMBRIDGE
UNIVERSITY PRESS

CAMBRIDGE UNIVERSITY PRESS
Cambridge, New York, Melbourne, Madrid, Cape Town, Singapore, São Paulo, Delhi

Cambridge University Press
32 Avenue of the Americas, New York, NY 10013–2473, USA

www.cambridge.org
Information on this title: www.cambridge.org/9780521666046

First published 2005
7th printing 2009

Printed in Hong Kong, China, by Golden Cup Printing Company Limited

A catalog record for this publication is available from the British Library

ISBN 978-0-521-66605-3 pack consisting of student's book and self-study audio CD/CD-ROM (Windows®, Mac®)
ISBN 978-0-521-60134-4 pack consisting of student's book/Korea and self-study audio CD/CD-ROM (Windows®, Mac®)
ISBN 978-0-521-60135-1 pack consisting of student's book A and self-study audio CD/CD-ROM (Windows®, Mac®)
ISBN 978-0-521-60136-8 pack consisting of student's book B and self-study audio CD/CD-ROM (Windows®, Mac®)
ISBN 978-0-521-66604-6 workbook
ISBN 978-0-521-60137-5 workbook A
ISBN 978-0-521-60138-2 workbook B
ISBN 978-0-521-66603-9 teacher's edition
ISBN 978-0-521-66600-8 CDs (audio)
ISBN 978-0-521-66601-5 cassettes

Art direction, book design, photo research, and layout services: Adventure House, NYC
Audio production: Full House, NYC

3 I'm Rudy.

| Grammar | Answer the questions. Write another piece of information.

1. Is Rudy from San Francisco?
   <u>No, he's not. He's from Los Angeles.</u>

2. Are his friends English majors?
   _____

3. Do his friends study in the evening?
   _____

4. Is he from a large family?
   _____

4 About you 2

| Grammar and vocabulary | Unscramble the questions. Then answer the questions with your own information.

1. name / What's / first / your ? <u>What's your first name?</u>
   _____

2. full-time / a / Do / have / you / job ? _____
   _____

3. live / best friend / Does / your / nearby ? _____
   _____

4. weekends / What / do / on / you / do ? _____
   _____

5. Where / you / for fun / go / do ? _____
   _____

6. teacher / your / like / What's ? _____
   _____

Things in common

1 What doesn't belong?

Vocabulary Circle the word that doesn't belong in each group.

1. apples (butter) mangoes strawberries
2. CD jacket jeans sweater
3. black color green red
4. baseball basketball singing volleyball
5. cat dog fish pet
6. dessert juice milk water

2 We're the same.

Grammar Respond to the statements with *too* or *either*.

1. I'm a soccer fan.

   I am too.

2. I can't stand doing the laundry.

   _____

3. I can sing karaoke all night.

   _____

4. I'm not a good cook.

   _____

5. I don't like shopping.

   _____

6. I love to swim in cold water.

   _____

3 First date

Grammar and vocabulary

**Complete the conversations with the expressions in the box.
Use each expression only once.**

✓I am too.	I do too.	I can too.	Me too.	Really?
I'm not either.	I don't either.	I can't either.	Me neither.	

David You know, I'm always nervous on first dates.

Lesley <u>I am too.</u>

David So, tell me about yourself, Lesley. What do you like to do?

Lesley Well, I go to rock concerts.

David _____ I'm a big fan of U2.

Lesley _____ They're my favorite group. I mean, I can listen to their music for hours.

David _____ Do you have all their CDs?

Lesley No, I don't. I don't have *All That You Can't Leave Behind*.

David _____ But I want to buy it.

Later

Lesley What do you on the weekends? I mean, do you eat out a lot?

David No. I don't usually go to restaurants.

Lesley _____ I like to eat at home.

David Oh, are you a good cook?

Lesley Um, not really.

David _____ But I like to cook.

Lesley Do you ever cook Italian food?

David Sure. But I'm allergic to cheese, so I can't eat pizza.

Lesley _____ I'm allergic to cheese, too!

David That's amazing! We have a lot in common. Do you like sports?

Lesley Uh, no, not at all.

David _____ I'm a big sports fan. I watch sports all weekend.

Lesley Huh. I can't stand sports.

4 About you

Grammar and vocabulary

Respond to these statements so they are true for you.

1. *A* I always eat chocolate for dinner.

   B <u>I do too.</u> **or** <u>Me too.</u> **or** <u>Really? I don't.</u>

2. *A* I'm not a baseball fan.

   B _____

3. *A* I can't drive.

   B _____

4. *A* I don't have a pet.

   B _____

5. *A* I'm allergic to bananas.

   B _____

6. *A* I can cook Italian food.

   B _____

Do you come here a lot?

1 Starting a conversation

Complete the conversations with the conversation starters in the box.

Is this your first English class here?   You look really nice today. That's a beautiful jacket.
Hey, I don't know you. Do you live around here?   Boy, the food is great. And this cake is really wonderful.
Is it me, or is it kind of noisy in here?   ✓Ooh, it's cold. Can I close the window?

1. A   <u>Ooh, it's cold. Can I close the window?</u>
   B   Sorry, I just opened it. I'm a little warm, actually.

2. A _____
   B   Thanks. Actually, it's from China.

3. A _____
   B   Thank you. It's my grandmother's recipe.

4. A _____
   B   Yes, it is. What about you?

5. A _____
   B   Yeah, it's pretty loud! Is this your first time here?

6. A _____
   B   Uh, no, I don't. I'm actually visiting from Guadalajara.

2 Um, actually, . . .

Conversation strategies

Circle the best response for each conversation starter.

1. I don't know anyone here. Do you?
   a. Um, actually, I know everybody.
   b. Actually, I don't know her.

2. So, are you British?
   a. Actually, where are you from?
   b. I'm Australian, actually.

3. Boy, it's hot today.
   a. Actually, I think it's OK.
   b. Well, actually, I do.

4. I like your jacket. Is it new?
   a. Actually, I like them, too.
   b. No, it's my sister's, actually.

5. This TV show is really interesting.
   a. It's a movie, actually.
   b. Actually, it was my grandfather's.

6. Do you work around here?
   a. No, I have a job, actually.
   b. Actually, I'm a full-time student.

7. It's a beautiful day. I love warm weather.
   a. You do, actually.
   b. Actually, I kind of like cold weather.

8. The bus is really late today.
   a. It's late every day, actually.
   b. Actually, it is late.

3 First day of class

Conversation strategies

Imagine it's the first day of English class. Respond to each conversation starter.

1. I don't know anyone here.   *Me neither. By the way, I'm James.*

2. This is a really big class. _____

3. Is it warm in here, or is it me? _____

4. Do you have a dictionary? _____

5. Are you a friend of Meg's? _____

6. I really like your cell phone. _____

7. Our teacher is really cool. _____

1 Getting together

Reading | **A** Look at the title of the article. Check (✓) the activities you think are in the article.

- ☐ do aerobics
- ☐ exercise at the gym
- ☐ get together and talk
- ☐ go shopping
- ☐ join a club
- ☐ listen to music
- ☐ play tennis
- ☐ take a dance class
- ☐ watch a movie

B Read the article. How many of your guesses in part A are correct?

World of Friends

Making Friends

Friends are important to all of us. They share our good days and our bad days. They are interested in us and our problems. But how do you make new friends? Here are some suggestions.

When you meet new people, find out what you have in common. Ask questions like, "What do you do in your free time?" or "What do you like to do on the weekends?" If you have things in common, you can do those activities together. It's fun to share your favorite activities with someone. If you both like movies, make a date to watch a movie. Or simply plan to get together one evening and talk – you don't have to spend money or go out to expensive places. Just spend time together.

But how can you meet new people? Think about your interests and the things you like to do. Do you have a hobby? Well, join a club. Do you want to learn to dance? Then sign up for a dance class. Start a conversation with people you meet at these places – you already have something in common.

When you start conversations with people, smile and be friendly. Make eye contact and don't forget to give compliments. People love to hear that they look nice or that you like their things, so be positive. Always listen to what the other person says, and ask follow-up questions.

When you make new friends, don't forget your old friends! Introduce your new friends to your old friends, too. After all, the more, the merrier!

C Read the article again. Match the two parts of each sentence.

1. Friends are important because __g__
2. Ask questions about general things _____
3. It's good to find out _____
4. It's not important to _____
5. Join clubs or take classes _____
6. Listen to the other person, _____
7. People love to hear _____

a. when you meet new people.
b. spend money – just spend time together.
c. and encourage him or her to talk.
d. nice things about themselves.
e. what activities you both like.
f. to meet people and make new friends.
g. they are interested in us and our problems.

2 Suggestions, please!

A Read this e-mail to Marcy, the editor of *Friends* magazine, and her reply. Correct the punctuation.

e-mail

dear marcy
what can I do i like to go out and do fun things but I don't know how to meet new people my friend says join a gym he's right but I don't like to exercise
ben

dear ben
what are your hobbies take up a new sport or hobby start conversations with people talk about general topics
marcy

e-mail

Dear Marcy,
What can I do?

B Read these questions. Write three suggestions for each question.

1. *Dave* I'd like to make friends, but I don't know how. Do you have any suggestions?

2. *Niki* I feel shy around new people. How can I improve my conversation skills?

Unit 1 Progress chart

Mark the boxes below to rate your progress. ✓ = I know how to . . . ? = I need to review how to . . .	To review, go back to these pages in the Student's Book.
Grammar	
☐ make statements with the simple present and with present of *be*	2, 3, 4, and 5
☐ ask questions with the simple present and present of *be*	2 and 3
☐ use *too* and *either* to agree	4 and 5
Vocabulary	
☐ name words to describe lifestyle, home and family, and work and studies	2 and 3
Conversation strategies	
☐ start conversations when meeting someone for the first time	6 and 7
☐ use *actually* to give and "correct" information	7
Writing	
☐ use correct punctuation	9

Unit 2 *Interests*

Leisure time

1 *What do they like to do?*

Grammar — Complete the sentences. Use the correct forms of the verbs in the box.

cook	dance	draw	play	✓read	work out

1. Pam and Victor aren't interested in ___reading___
   books. They both prefer ___to read___
   magazines. They really enjoy ___reading___
   fashion magazines.

2. Ian would like _____ every day. He
   doesn't like _____ in the gym at all.
   He enjoys _____ at home with a video.

3. Sun Hee can't _____ now. She's
   interested in _____ and would like
   _____ the tango.

4. Tom isn't good at _____ people.
   He can't _____ people at all, but
   he can _____ animals very well.

5. Amy and Dave usually like _____ ,
   but they hate _____ Italian food.
   They prefer _____ Chinese food.

6. Erica can't _____ the guitar very well.
   She enjoys _____ the guitar, but she's
   not very good at _____ it.

2 At home

Grammar Complete the conversation. Use the correct form of the verbs in the box.

bowl	go	ski	try
✓exercise	play	swim	watch

Linda You and I watch too much TV. We need some exercise.

James I know, but I don't really enjoy ___exercising___ .

Linda But you like _____ tennis, right?

James Yeah, but these days I prefer _____ tennis on TV.

Linda How about bowling? We can both _____ .

James Yeah, but it's always pretty noisy.

Linda I guess you're right.

James Well, you're good at _____ . And the pool is nearby.

Linda But it's always crowded.

James Oh, I know! We both like _____ .

Linda Actually, I can't stand the cold and snow.

James Really? Well, are you interested in _____ something new?

Linda Sure. I'd like _____ to the new Thai restaurant in our neighborhood.

James Great idea, Linda. Let's talk about exercise tomorrow.

3 About you

Grammar and vocabulary Answer the questions. Add more information.

1. *A* What are you good at?

   B <u>Well, I'm pretty good at learning languages. I can speak Portuguese and French.</u>

2. *A* Would you like to play a musical instrument?

   B _____

3. *A* What movie do you want to see?

   B _____

4. *A* Is there anything you really hate doing?

   B _____

5. *A* What activities do you enjoy doing on the weekends?

   B _____

6. *A* What are you bad at?

   B _____

1 All kinds of music

Vocabulary | Look at the pictures. Write the type of music.

1. ___folk music___

2. _____

3. _____

4. _____

5. _____

6. _____

7. _____

8. _____

2 What's new?

Grammar | Complete Kevin's e-mail with the correct pronouns.

○○○   **e-mail**

Hi Sam,

Guess what! My new job is at a music store. You know ___me___ (it / me) – I love listening to music. It's a great job, and I really like _____ (him / it).

So, what's cool right now? Well, the new Green Day CD is amazing! They're my favorite band. Do you like _____ (her / them)? My friends like Usher. Actually, almost _____ (everybody / nobody) I know is an Usher fan. But I don't really care for _____ (you / him). Gretchen Wilson is cool. Do you know _____ (her / us)? You like country music, right? You know, I actually kind of like _____ (it / them) now.

Oh, did I tell you? I'm in a band with my friends from the music store. They're really great. I want you to meet _____ (him / them). We play hip-hop. But my family never comes to listen to _____ (them / us) because (everyone / no one) _____ in my family likes hip-hop! But that's OK.

What's new with you? Write soon.

Kevin

3 Talking about music

Grammar | Complete the questions with object pronouns. Then answer the questions.

1. **A** Gwen Stefani is a great singer. She's pretty, too.
   Do you like __her__ ?
   B __Yes, I do. She's amazing.__

2. **A** You know Justin Timberlake, right? I think he's great.
   What do you think of _____ ?
   B _____

3. **A** You know, I'm not a fan of rap. How about you?
   Do you ever listen to _____ ?
   B _____

4. **A** Hey, the band Outkast performed on TV last night.
   They're really cool. Do you know _____ ?
   B _____

5. **A** My mom and dad love Sarah Chang. She's their
   favorite violinist. Do your parents like _____ ?
   B _____

6. **A** Do you like Latin music? Jeff and I have tickets for the
   Shakira concert. Do you want to go with _____ ?
   B _____

7. **A** I don't usually like country music, but I love the Dixie
   Chicks. Do you know _____ ?
   B _____

Gwen Stefani

Outkast

4 About you

Grammar and vocabulary | Answer the questions using object pronouns. Then give more information.

1. Do you like Alicia Keys? __Yes, I like her a lot. She has some great songs.__

2. What do you think of the Rolling Stones? _____

3. Do you like Mariah Carey? _____

4. Do you listen to pop music very often? _____

5. What do you think of folk music? _____

6. Do you and your friends ever go to concerts? _____

7. What do you think of Marc Anthony? _____

8. Do you know the band Destiny's Child? _____

I really like making things.

1 Saying no

Complete the conversations with the sentences in the box.

Um, no. He's lazy and just watches TV all day.   ✓ Not really. My mom knitted it for me last year.
Actually, no. My sister got it at the bakery.   No, but he has a big cap collection.
Well, no. I prefer to make peanut butter cookies.   No. I'm not really good with my hands.
Um, no, he just plays computer games!   Not really. He does crossword puzzles, though.

1. *Jenny*   I really like your sweater. Is it new?

   Keiko   <u>Not really. My mom knitted it for me last year.</u>

   Jenny   Can you knit or crochet?

   Keiko   _____ But I bake a little.

   Jenny   Oh, did you make this cake?

   Keiko   _____

   But I like to make cookies sometimes.

   Jenny   Me too. Do you ever make chocolate chip cookies?

   Keiko   _____

   My new boyfriend loves them!

2. *Mike*   I want to buy a Yankees baseball cap for my brother.

   Greg   Why? Is it his birthday?

   Mike   _____

   Does your brother collect anything?

   Greg   My brother? _____

   Mike   Really? Does he have *any* hobbies?

   Greg   _____

   Mike   Oh, yeah? My brother is on the computer all the time.

   Greg   Oh, does he do computer graphics?

   Mike   _____

2 No, not really.

Complete the responses to make them more friendly.

1. *A*   Are you into the Internet?

   B   Not really. <u>I don't have a computer.</u>

2. *A*   What a great photo! Are you interested in photography?

   B   No. _____

3. *A*   I really enjoy my piano lessons. Would you like to learn the piano?

   B   Um, no. _____

4. *A*   Look at these flowers. They're so beautiful. Do you enjoy gardening?

   B   Well, not really. _____

3 Yes and no

Answer the questions in a friendly way. Use *really* in each answer.

1. *A* Are you good at fixing things?

   B No, <u>not really. I'm not good with my hands.</u>

   C Yes. <u>I'm really good at fixing cars.</u>

2. *A* Do you make your own clothes?

   B No. _____

   C Yes, _____

3. *A* Does your best friend collect anything?

   B No, _____

   C Yes, _____

4. *A* Does your teacher speak Russian?

   B No, _____

   C Yes, _____

5. *A* Are you into winter sports, like skiing?

   B No, _____

   C Yes, _____

6. *A* Do you and your friends enjoy cooking?

   B Um, no. _____

   C Yes, _____

7. *A* Are your classmates into computer games?

   B No. _____

   C Yes, _____

8. *A* Are you interested in photography?

   B No. _____

   C Yes, _____

4 About you

Answer the questions with your own information. Use *really* in your answers.

1. Are you into sports?

   <u>Yes, I really like soccer and volleyball.</u> **or** <u>No, not really. I prefer to do something artistic.</u>

2. Would you like to learn a new skill?

   _____

3. Do you have a lot of hobbies?

   _____

4. Can you knit or sew?

   _____

5. Are you artistic?

   _____

1 Two popular hobbies

A Read the article. Check (✓) the pictures that the article describes.

☐ ☐ ☐

Young People's Hobbies

There are many hobbies and hobby sites on the Internet. Camping and chess sites are two of them. Although these two hobbies are very different, they have one thing in common: both are very popular with young people. Why?

One reason camping is so popular is because it's cheap. There are campgrounds around the world, and they're all different. Some have indoor swimming pools, restaurants, and game rooms. Others don't even have water! But the areas near campgrounds are almost always beautiful.

Camping is relaxing. Campers can get up early in the morning and cook breakfast with their friends or family. They can spend the day swimming, fishing, going hiking in the mountains, looking at wildlife, or just sitting in the sun. There's usually no noise, no traffic, and no stress. Campers usually sleep very well at night.

And what about chess? It's cool now, but in the past not many young people played the game. A lot of young people got interested in learning chess when they saw it in the first *Harry Potter* movie. And many celebrities enjoy playing chess. Bono, Moby, and Sting are all good at playing the game. Young people often follow what celebrities do, even if it's chess!

More and more schoolchildren are learning the game. Many schools have chess clubs, and there are national competitions every year. And people can play chess on computers, too. That means a person can compete against a computer, or can even play against another person on the Internet somewhere else in the world. You can play chess anywhere – even when you're camping!

B Read the article again. Then write **T** (true) or **F** (false) for each sentence. Correct the false sentences.

1. Camping and chess have nothing in common.   _F_   _They have one thing in common._

2. Camping is popular because it's cheap and stress-free. ____ _____

3. Campers hardly ever sleep well at night. ____ _____

4. Many young people played chess in the past. ____ _____

5. The first *Harry Potter* movie helped make camping popular. ____ _____

6. Many schools now have chess clubs. ____ _____

7. You can go camping on the Internet. ____ _____

2 My favorite hobby

Writing **A** Read about this hobby. Complete the sentences with *and*, *but*, *or*, *also*, or *because*.

○○○   Message Board

Rock climbing

One of my hobbies is rock climbing. I go once _____*or*_____ twice a month with my friends. We prefer to climb the mountains near my house _____ they are really beautiful. We usually go to Bear Mountain _____ to Kennedy Park. I prefer Kennedy Park _____ it's nearer. Kennedy Park _____ has a great campground.

It's great to be outdoors, _____ the weather isn't always very good. If it's raining _____ snowing, climbing can be very dangerous _____ the rocks get wet and slippery.

I can _____ go rock climbing indoors, especially during the winter. Sometimes my friends _____ I go climbing at the mall, _____ it's not the same. I just go once a month, usually on a Saturday _____ Sunday.

B Write about one of your hobbies.

One of my hobbies is

Unit 2 Progress chart

Mark the boxes below to rate your progress. ✓ = I know how to . . . ? = I need to review how to . . .	To review, go back to these pages in the Student's Book.
Grammar ☐ make statements with different verb forms	12 and 13
☐ ask questions with different verb forms	12 and 13
☐ use object pronouns, and the pronouns *everybody* and *nobody*	15
Vocabulary ☐ name at least 8 common interests	12 and 13
☐ name at least 8 hobbies	12, 13, 16, and 17
☐ name at least 8 kinds of music	14 and 15
Conversation strategies ☐ say *no* in a polite and friendly way	16 and 17
☐ use *really* and *not really* to make statements stronger or softer	17
Writing ☐ use *and*, *but*, *or*, *also*, or *because* to link ideas	19

Unit 3 Health

Healthy living

1 Staying in shape

Grammar Complete the conversations with the correct form of the verbs.

1. *Sandra* You ___look___ (look) great, Ashley. How ___do___
   you ___stay___ (stay) in shape?

   Ashley Well, I _____ (not eat) any junk food these days. And I
   usually _____ (exercise) three or four times a week.

   Sandra That's great. What kind of exercise _____ you usually
   _____ (do)? I mean, _____ you _____ (take)
   an aerobics class?

   Ashley No, but I just started a Latin dance class at Dance World.
   I really _____ (love) it. Actually, I _____ (walk)
   there now. _____ you _____ (want) to come?

   Sandra Uh, thanks, but I'm kind of busy right now.

   Ashley Really? Where _____ you _____ (go)?

   Sandra I _____ (go) to The Good Life.
   It's my favorite place to eat.

   Ashley Oh, is that a health-food restaurant?

   Sandra Actually, no, . . . it's an ice-cream store.

2. *Doctor* You're not in very good shape, Ken. Are you eating right?

   Ken Well, I _____ (want) to give up red meat, and
   I _____ (try) to eat a balanced diet, but it's hard.

   Doctor _____ you _____ (eat) a lot of vegetables
   these days?

   Ken Oh, yes. I _____ (eat) vegetables every day.
   I _____ (love) French fries.

   Doctor Oh. _____ you _____ (get) enough exercise
   these days?

   Ken To be honest, not really. I'm really busy.
   I _____ (take) a class three days a week.
   I _____ (learn) to bake cakes.

   Doctor But what about exercise? _____ you _____ (do)
   any exercise these days?

   Ken Well, I _____ (walk) to the video store every
   other day. And I _____ (play) pool twice a week.

2 Susan's lifestyle

Grammar | Look at the picture. Then answer the questions with the correct form
of the verbs in the box.

do karate	eat fruit	play tennis
✓drink water	exercise	try to lose weight

1. What is Susan doing now to stay healthy?

   a. ___She's drinking water.___

   b. _____

   c. _____

2. What else does she do to stay healthy?

   a. _____

   b. _____

   c. _____

3 About you

Grammar and vocabulary | Are these sentences true or false for you? Write *T* (true) or *F* (false).
Then correct the false statements.

1. __F__ I'm drinking a lot of milk these days.

   I'm not drinking a lot of milk these days. I'm drinking a lot of soda.

2. _____ My best friend eats junk food every other day.

   _____

3. _____ I'm not taking any classes right now.

   _____

4. _____ I sleep for five hours a night.

   _____

5. _____ My friends have a lot of stress in their lives.

   _____

6. _____ My family doesn't get any exercise at all.

   _____

1 What's the matter?

A There are seven health problems in the puzzle. Find the other six.
Look in these directions (↓→).

A	T	O	O	T	H	A	C	H	E	W	A
B	C	K	F	M	U	U	O	E	R	F	L
S	O	R	E	T	H	R	O	A	T	D	L
R	U	I	V	D	E	I	H	D	U	J	E
V	G	J	P	L	A	R	U	P	L	A	F
E	H	C	S	H	E	A	D	A	C	H	E
S	I	O	T	B	J	W	L	S	A	N	V
O	H	L	F	O	V	A	O	U	B	D	E
B	E	A	L	L	E	R	G	I	E	S	R
G	A	N	G	D	C	K	S	W	N	C	H
S	T	O	M	A	C	H	A	C	H	E	I
R	M	R	L	T	N	F	R	G	C	S	R

B Look at the picture. Write sentences with the words from part A.

Joe   Taro   Chad   Amy   Jim and Liz   Sara   Joyce

1. _Joe has a fever._
2. _____
3. _____
4. _____
5. _____
6. _____
7. _____

2 I feel sick.

Grammar and vocabulary

Look at the pictures. Write questions and answers.

Ann / the flu

Dan / a cold

1.   What does Ann do when she has the flu?
   When Ann has the flu, she stays in bed.

2. _____
   If _____

Rick / a headache

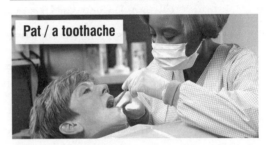

Pat / a toothache

3. _____
   _____ when _____

4. _____
   _____ if _____

3 About you

Grammar and vocabulary

Write questions for a friend using *when* or *if.* Then answer your friend's questions.

1.   *You*   What do you do when you're sick? _____
         (when / are sick)

   Friend   When I'm sick, I stay home and watch movies all day. How about you?

   You   _____

2.   *You*   _____
         (if / have a bad cough)

   Friend   I chat on the Internet instead of on the phone if I have a bad cough. And you?

   You   _____

3.   *You*   _____
         (if / get a stomachache)

   Friend   If I get a stomachache, I drink water. I don't eat a lot. How about you?

   You   _____

4.   *You*   _____
         (when / have a fever)

   Friend   When I have a fever, I take aspirin. I don't go out. What about you?

   You   _____

How come you're tired?

1 *It's my allergies.*

 Conversation strategies

Complete the conversation. Use the sentences in the box.

> Headaches too? Do you take anything?   ✓ Oh, no! Do you sneeze a lot?
> You're kidding! How come?   Gosh, that's terrible! So, what are you studying?
> Are you serious? You can't study?   Really? But how can you study when you feel sick?

Joan   What's the matter, Gary? Your nose and eyes are red.

Gary   Oh, it's my allergies. I always feel this way in the spring.

Joan   Oh, no! Do you sneeze a lot?

Gary   Oh, yes. I sneeze all the time. And I get headaches.

Joan   _____

Gary   Not really. Actually, I don't like to take medicine.

Joan   _____

Gary   Well, if I take medicine, I can't study.

Joan   _____

Gary   Well, you see, when I take medicine, I always fall asleep.

Joan   _____

Gary   It's hard, but I need to. I have a big test next week.

Joan   _____

Gary   I'm studying to be a doctor.

2 *You're kidding!*

Circle the best response to show surprise.

1. My wife talks in her sleep.
   a. My wife does too.
   (b.) Wow! What does she say?

2. I love getting up early on weekends.
   a. I always get up early.
   b. Early? I like to sleep late.

3. I take two or three naps every day.
   a. Oh! Are you sleeping enough at night?
   b. I know. And you snore, too.

4. I eat a lot of chocolate when I can't sleep.
   a. Me too. I love to eat chocolate at night.
   b. You're kidding! I can't sleep when
      I eat chocolate.

5. My grandfather goes running six days a week.
   a. No way! How old is he?
   b. I see. He's very healthy, right?

6. I often dream about food.
   a. I do too. I always dream about ice cream.
   b. Food? Are you hungry when you go to bed?

7. I have three part-time jobs.
   a. It's important to work hard.
   b. Really? Aren't you tired a lot?

8. If I can't sleep, I always listen to rock or hip-hop.
   a. Me too. I also listen to pop music.
   b. Gosh! Why not classical or jazz?

3 No way!

Write responses to show surprise. Then ask follow-up questions.

1. *A* My friends Chuck and Tina exercise when they can't sleep.

   B __No way!__ __What kind of exercise do they do?__

2. *A* My best friend never remembers her dreams.

   B _____ _____

3. *A* I sometimes sleep at the office.

   B _____ _____

4. *A* Sometimes I can't sleep because my dog snores.

   B _____ _____

5. *A* My brother has the same nightmare once a week.

   B _____ _____

6. *A* My father sleepwalks every night.

   B _____ _____

7. *A* I never use an alarm clock.

   B _____ _____

8. *A* My brother goes running right after he eats dinner.

   B _____ _____

4 About you

Answer the questions with your own information.

1. Are you feeling sleepy right now? _____

2. How often do you take naps on weekdays? _____

3. Do you ever sleep in class or at work? _____

4. Are you sleeping well these days? _____

5. What do you do when you wake up at night? _____

6. Do you dream in color? _____

Ways to relax

1 The practice of yoga

Reading **A** Read the article. Find the answers to these questions.

1. Where does yoga come from? _____
2. Is yoga good for stress? _____
3. Can you practice yoga alone? _____
4. Do children do yoga, too? _____

East Meets West

The ancient Eastern art of yoga is more than 5,000 years old. It's a combination of relaxation, stretching, breathing, a vegetarian diet, positive thinking, and meditation.

Yoga originated in India, but today it is becoming more and more popular in the United States. Why do Americans do yoga? One survey of yoga enthusiasts found out.

A majority (55%) of the people in the survey practice yoga because they want to relax. Some people do yoga to stay in shape. And other people do yoga when they feel depressed, have headaches, or have a lot of stress. Yoga is also helpful for people who have trouble sleeping.

What do people do when they practice yoga? Most of the people in the survey (90%) practice poses and breathing exercises. Half of them also meditate.

Where do Americans do yoga? Many people in the survey (48%) take classes at a local yoga studio. Others (39%) do it at home, either alone or with friends. A few people (9%) have a private teacher.

And how long do people do yoga? Most people in the survey (57%) do it for half an hour or an hour at a time. Some (41%) do yoga for an hour and a half. They all say it doesn't matter how often you do it – it's just important to do it. And it seems everyone is doing it these days. It's even popular with children!

Yoga keeps people healthy because it makes them strong and helps them relax, sleep, and cope with stress. So what about you? Would you like to try yoga?

B Read the article again. Then answer the questions.

1. What kind of diet do yoga teachers recommend? _a vegetarian diet_____
2. Why do Americans do yoga? Give three reasons. _____
3. What percentage of people in the survey practice poses and breathing? _____
4. Do most Americans in the survey do yoga at home? _____
5. According to the article, how long do most people do yoga? _____
6. Would you like to try yoga? Why or why not? _____

2 *Healthy lifestyles*

A Read these suggestions for a healthy lifestyle. Put in commas where necessary.

Healthy Habits

BY DR. GOODMAN

Take yoga classes. When you practice yoga**,** you stay in shape and relax at the same time.

If you can't sleep drink a glass of warm milk.

Sing at home or in your car if you want to have a lot of energy.

When you listen to music choose happy music.

If you have a headache take aspirin with a cup of hot tea.

Do something you love when you have a lot of stress.

B Choose a title and write a short article. Give three suggestions.

Sleep	Food and Diet	Exercise

Unit 3 Progress chart

Mark the boxes below to rate your progress. ✓ = I know how to . . . ? = I need to review how to . . .	To review, go back to these pages in the Student's Book.
Grammar	
☐ make statements with the simple present and present continuous	22 and 23
☐ ask questions with the simple present and present continuous	22 and 23
☐ use *if* and *when* in statements and questions	25
Vocabulary	
☐ name at least 8 healthy habits	22 and 23
☐ name at least 4 unhealthy habits	22 and 23
☐ name at least 6 health problems	24 and 25
Conversation strategies	
☐ keep a conversation going with comments and follow-up questions	26 and 27
☐ use expressions like *Wow!* or *You're kidding!* to show surprise	27
Writing	
☐ use commas in *if* and *when* clauses	29

Unit 4 Celebrations

Birthdays

1 What month is it?

Vocabulary **A** Write the months in the correct order.

_____ January _____ _____ _____

_____ _____ _____ _____

_____ _____ _____ _____

B Complete the sentences with the correct numbers.

1. January is the ___first___ month of the year.
2. March is the _____ month of the year.
3. June is the _____ month of the year.
4. July is the _____ month of the year.
5. October is the _____ month of the year.
6. December is the _____ month of the year.

2 When's her birthday?

Grammar and vocabulary Look at the dates. Then write each person's birthday two ways.

1. <u>Halle Berry's birthday is on August fourteenth.</u>
   <u>Halle Berry's birthday is on the fourteenth of August.</u>

2. _____
   _____

3. _____
   _____

4. _____
   _____

5. _____
   _____

6. _____
   _____

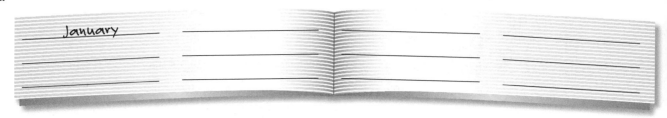

❶ Halle Berry 8/14

❷ Jackie Chan 4/7

❸ Jude Law 12/29

❹ Drew Barrymore 2/22

❺ Sofia Coppola 5/14

❻ Ronaldo 9/22

3 Future plans

Grammar **Complete the conversations with the correct form of *going to*.**

1. **Sam** What ___are you going to do___ (you / do) this weekend?

   Diane I _____ (see) my grandmother. We _____ (have) a birthday party for her.

   Sam That's nice. So, _____ (it / be) a big party?

   Diane No, not really. We _____ (not do) much. It _____ (be) just the family. Mom _____ (bake) her a cake. Then her friends _____ (take) her dancing. She's a tango teacher.

   Sam Your grandmother's a tango teacher? Cool.

2. **Yumi** That was Jun on the phone. He can't take us to Sarah's party.

   Kara Oh, no. Why not?

   Yumi No car. His parents are going to the mountains, and they _____ (take) the car.

   Kara Well, we can't drive. Who else _____ (be) there?

   Yumi Dan, but he _____ (not go) until after work.

   Kara Well, it looks like we _____ (walk). Wear comfortable shoes!

4 Happy birthday!

Grammar and vocabulary **Complete the card with the correct pronouns.**

Dear Kathleen,

Happy birthday! I'm sending ___you___ (you / her) this card from Mexico. Hector and I are in Mexico City visiting his parents. His parents are showing _____ (them / us) all the sights. His mother is so nice. I brought _____ (her / him) some jewelry from New York, and she wears it everywhere.

His mother is teaching _____ (you / me) how to make Mexican food. She's going to send _____ (them / us) a tamale pot when we get home. Hector loves tamales, so I can make _____ (him / her) tamales next Christmas. We want to do something special for his parents, but we can't give _____ (us / them) anything because they won't let us!

How about you? Can I bring _____ (you / me) anything from Mexico for your birthday?

Ellen

27

1 Good times

Vocabulary Look at the pictures. Write the special event. Then complete the descriptions with the expressions in the box.

blow out the candle	go out for a romantic dinner	shout "Happy New Year"
exchange rings	go trick-or-treating	✓ sing "Happy Birthday"
get a diploma	have a reception	✓ wear a cap and gown
give her chocolates	see fireworks	wear costumes

graduation day

birthday

1. Ana and her classmates are going to __wear a cap and gown__ . When they call her name, Ana's going to _____ .

2. The waiters are going to __sing "Happy Birthday"__ and bring Erin a cake. She's going to make a wish and

_____ .

3. Allen and Carine are going to

_____ .

After dinner, Allen's going to

_____ .

4. Bruce and Sheila are going to a big party. They're going to _____ on the beach. Then at midnight, they're going to _____ .

5. Ahmad and Keisha are going to get married. During the wedding, they're going to _____ . After the wedding, they're going to

_____ .

6. John and Rudy are going to _____ of their favorite comic-book characters. When they're ready, they're going to _____ in the neighborhood.

2 A busy week

Grammar | Read George's calendar. Write a sentence about each plan. Use the present continuous.

May						
Sunday	Monday	Tuesday	Wednesday	Thursday	Friday	Saturday
8 Mother's Day - Have lunch with Mom.	9 **8:00** - Meet Ann for dinner.	10 Tennis after work	11 Lunch with Joe	12 Yoga before work	13 **2:00** - Go to Keith and Karen's wedding.	14 **5:00** - Go to Jennifer's graduation party.

1. <u>On May eighth, George is having lunch with his mother.</u>
2. _____
3. _____
4. _____
5. _____
6. _____
7. _____

3 What's going to happen?

Grammar | Write a prediction about each picture. Use *going to* or *not going to*.

1. <u>It's not going to be sunny.</u>
   (sunny)
2. _____
   (trick-or-treating)
3. _____
   (flowers)

4. _____
   (fireworks)
5. _____
   (diploma)
6. _____
   (snow)

1 "Vague" expressions

Conversation strategies

Complete the conversations. Use *and everything* or *and things (like that)*. Leave two blanks empty in each conversation.

1. *Maya* What are you doing on New Year's?

   Brittany Well, my family's having dinner at my grandmother's house _____ . You know, a big dinner with ham and mashed potatoes ___and everything___ .

   Maya Sounds great! Do you have pies _____ ?

   Brittany Yeah, but I'm trying to lose weight. There's all this holiday food like cookies _____ . It's really hard to be on a diet.

   Maya Yeah, I have the same problem. And I work at a bakery _____ . So let's enjoy the holidays and diet next year.

   Brittany Great idea! I'm hungry. Let's go out and eat some cake, ice cream, _____ .

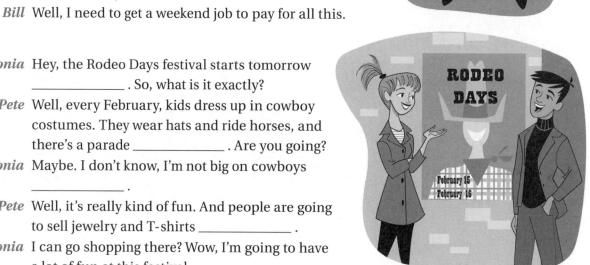

2. *Carol* Can we do something romantic for our anniversary this year _____ ? Can you give me chocolates, send me flowers, _____ ?

   Bill Sure, I can do that _____ .

   Carol And I'd like to go out for a nice dinner.

   Bill Well, it depends. Where do you want to go?

   Carol Somewhere with violin music and candles _____ .

   Bill OK. . . . Uh, do you want a present, too?

   Carol Of course! I'd like some jewelry, some clothes, _____ .

   Bill Oh. When's our anniversary again?

   Carol On the twenty-fifth.

   Bill Well, I need to get a weekend job to pay for all this.

3. *Sonia* Hey, the Rodeo Days festival starts tomorrow _____ . So, what is it exactly?

   Pete Well, every February, kids dress up in cowboy costumes. They wear hats and ride horses, and there's a parade _____ . Are you going?

   Sonia Maybe. I don't know, I'm not big on cowboys _____ .

   Pete Well, it's really kind of fun. And people are going to sell jewelry and T-shirts _____ .

   Sonia I can go shopping there? Wow, I'm going to have a lot of fun at this festival _____ .

2 About you

Conversation strategies

Answer the questions with the responses in the box. Use each response only once. Then add more information or a follow-up question.

| It depends. | Maybe. | ✓ I don't know. | I'm not sure. |

1. Are you going to celebrate your birthday with a party and everything?

   I don't know. My girlfriend usually surprises me on my birthday.

2. What do you want to do this weekend?

   _____

3. Are you going to send your mom some flowers on her birthday?

   _____

4. Do you want to go see the fireworks tonight?

   _____

3 Scrambled conversation

Conversation strategies

Number the lines of the conversation in the correct order.

☐ But you can also shop for cool Chinese gifts and things.

[1] Would you like to go to a Chinese festival?

☐ OK. So, what do people do?

☐ There's going to be free food? Great, I'd love to go.

☐ Well, I don't know. I'm not big on dances and stuff like that.

☐ Well, at least the food is great, and it's free.

☐ Uh, maybe, but I don't have money for shopping right now.

☐ It's for Chinese New Year.

☐ Lots of things, like lion dances and everything!

☐ I'm not sure. What kind of festival is it exactly?

1 Celebrating mothers

Reading **A** Read the article. Then add the correct heading to each paragraph.

Traditional ways to celebrate   History of the holiday   When is Mother's Day?
Ideas for Mother's Day   ✓ Why people celebrate Mother's Day

Mother's Day

Why people celebrate Mother's Day

In many countries, there is a special day of the year when children of all ages celebrate their mothers. On this day – Mother's Day – children tell their mothers that they love them, and thank them for their love and care.

_____

Mother's Day is not a new celebration. Historians say that it started as a spring festival in ancient Greece. The modern festival of Mother's Day probably comes from England in the 1600s, when people had a day off from their jobs to visit their mothers on a day they called "Mothering Sunday." They took small gifts and a special cake called "simnel cake." In the United States, Mother's Day became an official holiday in 1914.

_____

People in different countries celebrate Mother's Day on different days. In Australia, Brazil, Italy, Japan, Turkey, and the United States, it's on the second Sunday in May, whereas in France and Sweden, it's on the last Sunday in May. In Argentina, Mother's Day is celebrated on the second Sunday in October, whereas in Spain and Portugal, it's on December 8.

_____

Although many countries celebrate Mother's Day at different times of the year, the holidays have one purpose in common – to show love and appreciation for mothers. For example, on Mother's Day morning, some children bring their mothers breakfast in bed. Others give their mothers gifts they made especially for this holiday. And adults buy their mothers flowers or send them cards.

_____

What are you going to do next Mother's Day? Maybe you can use some of these ideas to make your mother feel special.

- _make or buy your mother a beautiful Mother's Day card_
- _write her a letter telling her why you appreciate her_
- _do a special chore for her_
- _make her a special meal or bake a cake_
- _buy her some flowers or her favorite candy_
- _plant a flower or tree somewhere she can see it_

B Read the article again. Answer the questions.

1. Where did the idea of Mother's Day come from originally? _____

2. Which country started the tradition of giving presents on Mother's Day? _____

3. What was Mother's Day called in England? _____

4. When do Brazil and Japan celebrate Mother's Day? _____

5. What are three traditions on Mother's Day? _____

_____

2 *Making plans*

Writing **A** Start and end these notes to different people.

A note to a friend	A message to your neighbor	A letter to your teacher
Hi Steve,	_____	_____
I'm having a party on Saturday night. Everybody's going to be there. Hope you can make it.	I'm having a party on Friday. We're going to have a band. I hope it's not too noisy. Please join us.	I can't come to class tomorrow. I have a fever and a headache, so my mother is taking me to the doctor.
See you then.	_____	_____

B Write to these people about a special celebration.

A note to a teacher	A message to a friend	A letter to your grandparents

Unit 4 Progress chart

Mark the boxes below to rate your progress. ☑ = I know how to . . . ? = I need to review how to . . .	To review, go back to these pages in the Student's Book.
Grammar ☐ use *going to* for the future ☐ use indirect objects and indirect object pronouns ☐ use the present continuous for specific future plans	35, 36, and 37 34 and 35 37
Vocabulary ☐ name the months of the year ☐ name the days of the month (ordinal numbers 1–31)	34 and 35 34 and 35
Conversation strategies ☐ use "vague" expressions like *and everything* and *and things* ☐ use "vague" responses like *Maybe* and *It depends*	38 and 39 39
Writing ☐ start and end invitations and personal notes	41

Unit 5 Growing up

Childhood

1 What's the year?

Vocabulary Write the years in numbers or words.

1. twenty ten _____2010_____
2. nineteen oh-four _____
3. two thousand eight _____
4. nineteen seventy-seven _____
5. 1982 _____nineteen eighty-two_____
6. 2006 _____
7. 2013 _____
8. 1998 _____

2 Talking about the past

Grammar Complete the conversations with *was, wasn't, were, weren't, did,* or *didn't.*

1. *Rick* So, Dina, ___did___ you grow up here in Miami?

   Dina Yes, I _____ , but we _____ born here.
   My sister and I _____ born in Puerto Rico,
   and we moved here when we _____ kids.

   Rick _____ you study English when you _____
   in school in Puerto Rico?

   Dina Yes, we _____ – for a few years – but we _____
   really learn English until we came here.

   Rick Wow! And now you speak English better
   than I do – and I _____ born here!

2. *Thomas* When ___were___ you born, Grandma?

   Grandma I _____ born in 1929.

   Thomas Really? _____ you born here in Los Angeles?

   Grandma No, I _____ . Your grandfather and I _____
   both born in China.

   Thomas So when _____ you come to the U.S.?

   Grandma My family _____ move here until I _____
   13 years old.

   Thomas _____ you go to school in China?

   Grandma No, I _____ . My parents _____ rich,
   so I had to work.

   Thomas And when _____ Grandpa born?

   Grandma He _____ born in 1928, but he says
   he _____ really born until 1947.

   Thomas Why does he say that?

   Grandma Because that's when he met *me*.

3 A life story

Grammar Complete the story with the words in the box. You can use some words more than once.

✓ago	for	from	in	last	long	then	to	until	when

This is a picture of my best friend, Mi Young. I took it a few years __ago__ .
Mi Young and I met _____ 1988. We were very young _____ we became
friends. Mi Young is a very interesting person. She was born in Busan, South
Korea, _____ 1984. Her family moved to the U.S. _____ she was three
years old. They lived in Chicago _____ Mi Young was fifteen. _____ they
moved to New York City. I cried _____ a long time after they moved.

Mi Young didn't live in New York _____ because she came back to Chicago for **college**
_____ she was eighteen. We were roommates at the University of Chicago _____ four years –
_____ 2001 _____ 2004. We graduated _____ year. Eight months _____ , Mi Young got a great
job in Phoenix, Arizona, and moved there. I really miss her! But guess what? Two months _____ ,
I got a job there, too. I'm moving there _____ two weeks, and I can't wait!

4 About you

Grammar and vocabulary Unscramble the questions. Then answer the questions with your own information.

1. you / When / born / were ? _When were you born?_ _____

2. Where / born / your / were / parents ? _____

3. grow up / you / Where / did ? _____

4. best friend / Who / your / was / ago / five years ? _____

5. a child / you / move / when / Did / ever / were / you ? _____

6. you / play video games / Did / when / you / little / were ? _____

7. long / you / were / elementary school / How / in ? _____

Favorite classes

1 What's the subject?

A Circle the word that doesn't belong. Then write the general category of the subjects.

1. history	(chemistry)	economics	geography	*social studies*
2. gymnastics	dance	art	track	_____
3. geometry	computer studies	algebra	calculus	_____
4. literature	biology	chemistry	physics	_____
5. choir	band	drama	orchestra	_____

B Complete the crossword puzzle.

Across

1. In this math subject, you see the letters *x* and *y* a lot.
7. I can run fast and jump high. I'm good at this P.E. subject.
8. Students sing in this music class.
9. In this subject, you study about people and things from a long time ago.
10. Students learn to be actors when they study this subject.

Down

2. In this class, you study the countries of the world and their oceans, rivers, and mountains.
3. You draw and paint in this class.
4. This subject is a science. You learn about plant and animal life.
5. In this subject, teachers ask students to read novels, stories, and poems.
6. In this class, students play classical music on instruments.

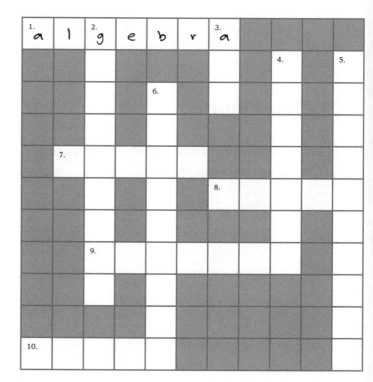

2 *How did we do?*

Grammar **A** Write the determiners in order in the chart below.

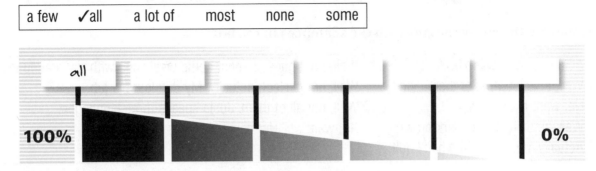

| a few | ✓all | a lot of | most | none | some |

B Read the test results. Complete the sentences with the determiners in the box. Use each expression only once.

	Chemistry	English	Geography	Geometry
Passed	55%	100%	90%	15%
Failed	45%	0%	10%	85%

| A few | A few of | All of | A lot of | Most of | None of | ✓Some | Some of |

1. ____Some____ students in the class passed chemistry. _____ them failed chemistry.
2. _____ the students passed English. _____ the students failed it.
3. _____ the students passed geography. _____ students failed it.
4. _____ the students passed geometry. _____ people failed it.

3 *About you*

Grammar and vocabulary Answer the questions. Write true sentences using determiners.

When you were in high school, what was a subject . . .

1. most of your friends liked? <u>Most of my friends liked P.E.</u> _____
2. all of the students had to study? _____
3. a lot of students hated? _____
4. some of your classmates loved? _____
5. no students ever failed? _____
6. a few students were always really good at? _____
7. none of your classmates liked? _____
8. a lot of students got good grades in? _____
9. some students dropped? _____

Well, actually, . . .

1 Correcting things you say

Complete the conversations with the sentences in the box.

Actually, no, it was 2002. Well, no, I guess I spent some weekends with my grandparents.
Well, at least most of them didn't. Well, not perfect, actually. My dad lost his job.
No, wait. I was nine. ✓Well, not all of them. Josie speaks three languages.
Well, actually, it was dark brown. No, wait. . . . Her name was Mrs. Santos.
Actually, no, I was 18 when I quit.

1. *A* All my friends are bilingual. They all speak two languages.

    Well, not all of them. Josie speaks three languages.

    B That's amazing!

2. *A* My best friend and I had sleepovers every weekend when we were kids.

    _____

    B That sounds like fun.

3. *A* We moved to Rio de Janeiro when I was ten.

    _____

    B So you were pretty young.

4. *A* I was on a swimming team until I was 16.

    _____

    B That's the reason you swim so well.

5. *A* My brother and I had a perfect childhood.

    _____

    B Really? But you were generally pretty happy, right?

6. *A* My cousin lived with us for a year – in 2003, I think.

    _____

    B That was your cousin Alice, right?

7. *A* My favorite teacher in elementary school was Mrs. Santana.

    _____

    B Oh, yeah? My favorite teacher was Mr. Stiller.

8. *A* When I was little, none of my friends had pets.

    _____

    B But you had a dog, right?

9. *A* I had black hair when I was born.

    _____

    B Really? I was born with no hair at all!

2 I mean

Conversation strategies

Complete the questions using *I mean* to correct the underlined words. Then answer the questions.

1. When you were a child, what was the name of your first <u>professor</u>, _I mean, teacher_ ?

   _____

2. Were you six or seven when you started <u>high school</u>, _____ ?

   _____

3. In elementary school, did you have lunch in the school <u>café</u>, _____ ?

   _____

4. As a kid, what was your favorite <u>sport</u>, _____ ?

   Did you like checkers? _____

5. When you were young, did you play any <u>music</u>, _____ , like the piano?

   _____

3 About you

Conversation strategies

Complete these sentences so they are true for you.

1. I started school when I was three. Actually, no,
   when I was five .

2. The name of my elementary school was Park Elementary.
   No, wait. . . . _____ .

3. My first teacher's name was Miss Parker, I mean,
   _____ .

4. I always got good grades in every subject.
   Well, _____ .

5. Most of my childhood friends liked classical music.
   Well, no, _____ .

6. When I was a child, my favorite holiday was Halloween,
   I mean, _____ .

7. I remember all my classmates in kindergarten.
   Well, actually, _____ .

8. A lot of my friends did gymnastics after school.
   No, wait. . . . _____ .

1 Small-town story

Reading **A** Read the story of Yolanda's life. Then number the pictures in the correct order.

INTERVIEW: *A happy childhood* by *Kathy Montaño*

Kathy Montaño grew up in the small town of Bagdad, Arizona. She interviewed several Mexican Americans in Bagdad about their childhood. This is the story of Yolanda Sandoval.

"My name is Yolanda Sandoval. I was born in Cananea, Mexico, on June 13, 1922. My parents brought me to Bagdad when I was six months old. My father's name was Francisco Sandoval, and my mother's name was Cecilia Bernal.

I was their first child. I have four younger brothers. My mother gave Rafael, my third brother, her name as a middle name. Apart from Rafael, no one had a middle name. My mother was very gentle and patient. She died when I was 16. My father was very kind but strict.

What did my father do for a living? He worked in a mine. He didn't talk much about his work, maybe because he didn't like it. My mother didn't go to work. She stayed home to take care of us.

My mother always did special things for our birthdays. One year she gave me a purple party. Everything was purple, even the drinks! She also made me a purple dress. That was the best party I ever had. I invited all my friends – except for Bobby. I was angry with him at the time.

My brothers and I loved the movies. We thought they were wonderful. A man named Angel Ruiz always showed old cowboy movies at the local theater, and we went to all of them. He charged five cents for a movie. Sometimes we didn't have the five cents, but he let us see the movie anyway.

What about school? What subjects did I study? I had to study English for four years, science for two (I took chemistry and biology), and a foreign language for two years. I took Spanish, of course! Spanish was easy for me, so I got good grades. I also studied U.S. history, home economics, and physical education. I loved school!"

B Read Yolanda's story again. Then complete the sentences.

1. Kathy Montaño interviewed several people in her town about _____ .

2. Yolanda Sandoval came to Bagdad when she _____ .

3. Yolanda's father didn't talk much about his work because _____ .

4. On Yolanda's birthday one year, her mother gave her _____ .

5. At the local movie theater, Yolanda and her brothers saw _____ .

6. Yolanda studied English for _____ .

2 When I was a teenager

Writing **A** Answer these questions about your first year in high school. Use *except (for)* or *apart from.*

1. Did you like your teachers?

   <u>I liked all my teachers except for my history teacher, Mr. Crown.</u>

2. Did you get along with your parents?

   _____

3. Did you enjoy your high school subjects?

   _____

4. Did you get along with all your classmates?

   _____

5. Did you and your best friend do a lot of things together?

   _____

B Write about some of your favorite activities when you were a teenager.

When I was a teenager, I lived in

My friends and I loved to

Unit 5 Progress chart

Mark the boxes below to rate your progress. ☑ = I know how to . . . ? = I need to review how to . . .	To review, go back to these pages in the Student's Book.
Grammar	
☐ make statements and ask questions with the simple past and past of *be*	44 and 45
☐ talk about the past using time expressions	44 and 45
☐ use determiners: *all (of), most (of), a lot of, some (of), a few (of), no, none of*	46 and 47
Vocabulary	
☐ say years	44 and 45
☐ name at least 12 school subjects	47
☐ name at least 5 general subject categories	47
Conversation strategies	
☐ correct things I say with expressions like *Actually* and *No, wait*	48 and 49
☐ use *I mean* to correct myself	49
Writing	
☐ use *except (for)* and *apart from* to link ideas	51

Unit 6 Around town

Out shopping

1 Where . . . ?

Grammar and vocabulary

Look at the map. Write two answers for each question.

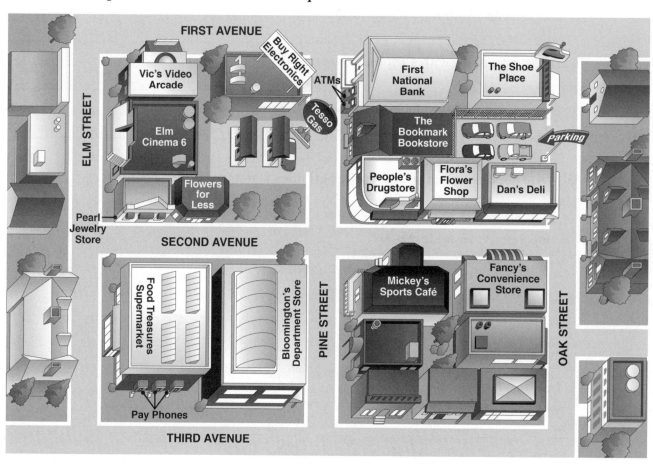

1. Where's the bookstore?   It's on Pine Street, between the bank and the drugstore.
   It's across the street from the gas station.

2. Where are the pay phones?   _____

   _____

3. Where's the parking lot?   _____

   _____

4. Where are the ATMs?   _____

   _____

5. Where's the gas station?   _____

   _____

6. Where's the drugstore?   _____

   _____

2 *Looking for places*

Grammar | Write questions. Then complete the answers with *there's one, there are some, there isn't one,* or *there aren't any.*

1. A <u>Is there a drugstore around here?</u> _____ (drugstore / around here ?)
   B Yes, <u>there's one</u> on the corner of Pine Street and Second Avenue.

2. A _____ (parking lot / near here ?)
   B _____ on Oak Street, behind the bookstore.

3. A _____ (video arcades / anywhere ?)
   B _____ over there, next to the electronics store.

4. A _____ (museum / in this town ?)
   B No, sorry, _____ .

5. A _____ (public restrooms / near here ?)
   B No, _____ public restrooms near here, but there are some
   inside the department store on Pine Street.

6. A _____ (pay phones / around here ?)
   B Yeah, sure, _____ on Third Avenue.

3 *About you*

Grammar and vocabulary | Write questions. Then answer the questions about your neighborhood.

1. A (a good coffee shop) <u>Is there a good coffee shop in this neighborhood?</u>
   B <u>Yes, there is. There's Emily's on the corner of Center Avenue and First Street.</u>

2. A (a big department store) _____
   B _____

3. A (any Internet cafés) _____
   B _____

4. A (a convenience store) _____
   B _____

5. A (any cheap restaurants) _____
   B _____

1 Places in town

Vocabulary Complete the sentences with the places in the box.

✓aquarium	museum	running path	stadium	visitors' center
hotel	parking garage	skateboard ramp	theater	water park

You can . . .

1. see sea animals at an _aquarium_ .
2. swim in an outdoor pool at a _____ .
3. go jogging on a _____ .
4. go skateboarding on a _____ .
5. see a play at a _____ .

6. see art and interesting old things at a _____ .
7. ask for information at a _____ .
8. leave your car at a _____ .
9. watch a baseball game at a _____ .
10. sleep at a _____ .

2 Where am I going?

Vocabulary Some people are at the Sea View Hotel. Where do they want to go? Look at the map. Complete the conversations with the names of the places.

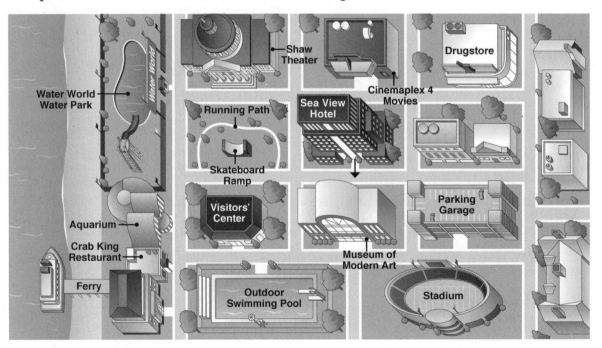

1. *A* Can you tell me how to get to the _____ ?
   B Sure. When you leave the hotel, turn right. It's on the next block. It's there on your right.

2. *A* Can you tell me how to get to the _____ ?
   B Yes. Go out of the hotel, and turn left. Turn left again at the corner, go one block, and turn right. It's on your left.

3. *A* Can you help me? I'd like to go to the _____ .
   B Yes. Turn right out of the hotel. Go straight for another block, and make a left. Walk two blocks. It's on your right, next to the restaurant.

3 Directions, directions

Rewrite the sentences to make requests. Then look at the map on page 44, and write directions.

1. You're at the Visitors' Center. "Tell me how to get to the museum."(Could)

   A _Could you tell me how to get to the museum?_

   B _Turn left. Walk straight ahead for a block._

   The museum is going to be right there on the left.

2. You're at the museum. "Give me directions to the aquarium." (Could)

   A _____

   B _____

3. You're at the aquarium. "Tell me how to get to the pool." (Can)

   A _____

   B _____

4. You're at the pool. "Recommend a good place for skateboarding." (Can)

   A _____

   B _____

5. You're at the skateboard ramp. "Give me directions to the Visitors' Center." (Can)

   A _____

   B _____

4 Can you help me?

Write requests and offers.

1. Make an offer: Ask how you can help the person.

   How can I help you?

2. Make a request: Ask for directions to the aquarium.

   _____

3. Make a request: Ask for help.

   _____

4. Make an offer: Ask someone what you can do.

   _____

5. Make a request: Ask someone to recommend a good place to go running.

   _____

Excuse me?

1 Checking information

Complete the conversations. Check the information.

1. *A* Hi. Where to?

   B I'm going to 830 Center Street.

   A <u>I'm sorry? Did you say 813 Center Street?</u>

   B No, 830. That's on the corner of Center and Main – on the left side of the street.

   A _____

   B Yes, the left side.

2. *A* Could you tell me how to get to Atlantic Bank?

   B _____

   A Yes. Do you know it?

   B I think so. Go straight ahead for three blocks, and turn left. The bank is on the right.

   A _____

   B No. Turn left. The bank is on the right.

3. *A* Can I help you?

   B Yes, please. What time does the next show start?

   A At 7:15.

   B _____

   A 7:15.

   B And what time does it end?

   A It ends at 9:05.

   B _____

   A Yes, that's right.

4. *A* Can you give me directions to a pet store?

   B _____

   A No, not a bookstore – a pet store. I want to buy some new fish for my aquarium.

   B Oh. Let me think. I think there's a pet store at Bay Street Mall.

   A _____

   B Bay Street Mall. It's about half an hour from here.

2 Questions, questions

Write an "echo" question for the underlined expression in each conversation.

1. *A* The concert tickets cost <u>sixty dollars each</u>.
   B <u>They cost how much?</u>

2. *A* There's a <u>great bicycle path</u> in the park.
   B _____

3. *A* The stadium is <u>on State Street</u>.
   B _____

4. *A* The aquarium closes at <u>8:30</u> on Friday nights.
   B _____

5. *A* Let's go to the museum. It's <u>just a few blocks away</u>.
   B _____

3 I'm sorry?

Complete the "echo" question in each conversation.

1. *A* A new deli opened right across the street from us.
   B I'm sorry, a new __what__ opened?
   A A new deli.
   B Great! Now I don't have to cook!

2. *A* Tim spent almost five hundred dollars on theater tickets for his family.
   B Excuse me? He spent _____ ?
   A Almost five hundred dollars.
   B Wow! I hope the play's good!

3. *A* I really want to leave at 6:00.
   B Sorry? You want to leave at _____ ?
   A At 6:00.
   B Uh-oh. We're late!

4. *A* Howard is going to the aquarium today.
   B I'm sorry? He's going _____ ?
   A To the aquarium. You know, the one on Main Street.
   B Oops! I told him I'd meet him there.

1 Life down under

Reading

A Look at the pictures. Check (✓) the items you think the article talks about.

☐ an amusement park
☐ an underground hotel
☐ a rock and roll museum

☐ a place that looks like the moon
☐ a drive-in movie theater
☐ an opal mine

B Read the article. How many of your guesses in part A are correct?

Coober Pedy

Coober Pedy – the Opal Capital of the World

Welcome to the desert town of Coober Pedy in the outback of Australia. The name Coober Pedy comes from the Aboriginal words *kupa piti*, which mean "white man in a hole." We hope you'll come visit.

opal

Explorers first found opals in this area on February 1, 1915. In 1946, an Aboriginal woman named Tottie Bryant dug out a large and valuable opal. After that, a lot of people came to Coober Pedy to mine opals.

During the 1960s, many European immigrants came to work here, and Coober Pedy quickly became a large modern town. Today, Coober Pedy is the world's main source of high-quality opals and a unique tourist spot.

It's so hot in Coober Pedy that a lot of people live underground!

There are many underground homes, as well as underground hotels, museums, opal shops, art galleries, and, of course, opal mines.

We recommend that you visit these places when you come to Coober Pedy:

The Opal Mine & Museum is a unique underground museum about the history of the town. It includes a model underground home and a small opal mine. Some of the world's finest opals are on display here.

The Moon Plain is a large rocky area unlike anywhere else. It looks like the moon – or another planet! It was the set for many movies, including *Mad Max Beyond Thunderdome; The Adventures of Priscilla, Queen of the Desert*; and *The Red Planet.* It is about 15 kilometers northeast of Coober Pedy.

Coober Pedy Drive-In is an open-air movie theater. You can see four movies a month here – every other weekend on Friday and Saturday nights.

C Read the article on Coober Pedy again. Then match the two parts of each sentence.

1. The name Coober Pedy means __d__
2. Tottie Bryant found ____
3. Coober Pedy became a modern mining town when ____
4. At present, Coober Pedy is the world's main source ____
5. As a tourist place, Coober Pedy is famous for ____
6. The Moon Plain was ____

a. the set for many movies.
b. a very big and valuable opal.
c. its underground homes, museums, stores, and mines.
d. "white man in a hole."
e. immigrants came to work in the mines.
f. of high-quality opals.

2 Walking guide

Writing **A Read this New Orleans walking tour. Look at the map, and fill in the missing words.**

Start at #1. This is the Garden District Book Shop. Anne Rice, a famous author from New Orleans, calls this her favorite bookstore.

Now go to #2. Take Prytania Street __four__ blocks to Philip Street. Turn _____ on Philip Street. Take Philip Street one _____ to Coliseum Street. _____ a right on Coliseum Street. They're on the _____ . These homes are called the Seven Sisters. A man wanted his seven daughters to live close to him. He built these seven houses for them as wedding gifts.

Now go to #3. Go _____ on Coliseum Street, and walk to the end of the block. _____ left on First Street. Go _____ for one block. It's right there, on the _____ . This is the Brevard-Mahat-Rice House, where Anne Rice lives and works.

B Think of two tourist attractions in your town or city. Write directions from one to the other.

Start at

Unit 6 Progress chart

Mark the boxes below to rate your progress. ✓ = I know how to . . . ? = I need to review how to . . .	To review, go back to these pages in the Student's Book.
Grammar	
☐ use *Is there?* and *Are there?* to ask about places in a town	54 and 55
☐ use *across from*, *behind*, *between*, etc., to describe location	55
☐ make offers and requests with *Can* and *Could*	56 and 57
Vocabulary	
☐ name at least 15 places in a city or town	54, 55, and 56
Conversation strategies	
☐ check information by repeating key words and using "checking" expressions	58 and 59
☐ ask "echo" questions to check information	59
Writing	
☐ write a guide giving directions	61

Unit 7 Going away

Getting ready

1 What are they going to do?

Grammar and vocabulary

A Match the sentences.

1. Jim and Ann are planning to go to Ecuador. _d_
2. First, Jim needs to call the embassy. _____
3. Then he's going to go on the Internet. _____
4. Ann has to go to a bookstore. _____
5. Then she's going to the library. _____
6. Jim's going to go to the bank. _____
7. Jim and Ann are going to go to the mall. _____
8. They're going to the bus station. _____

a. He needs to find out about visas.
b. She wants to buy a good guidebook.
c. They want to pick up an airport bus schedule.
d. They're going to learn Spanish.
e. He's going to look for a cheap flight online.
f. They have to buy some suitcases.
g. He needs to change some money.
h. She wants to do research before they go.

B Combine the sentences. Write one sentence for each pair of sentences in part A.

1. _Jim and Ann are planning to go to Ecuador to learn Spanish._
2. _____
3. _____
4. _____
5. _____
6. _____
7. _____
8. _____

50

2 Reasons for getting away

Grammar Match the expressions with the plans and reasons. Then write the sentences.

Plan		Reason
I'm planning	to go online	to buy train tickets
I'm going	to go to Chile	to go snorkeling
I want	to go to the beach	to go skiing
I'd like	to fly to Shanghai	to try the regional food
I need	to eat at local restaurants	to learn some expressions
I'm not going	to get a Korean phrase book	to see old friends

1. I'm planning to go to the beach to go snorkeling.

2. _____

3. _____

4. _____

5. _____

6. _____

3 Message board

Grammar Complete the questions on the message board. Then answer the questions with true information about your town or city.

Visitors' Center Message Board

1. **From:** clueless Is it important to bring a guidebook ? (important / bring a guidebook)

   From: travelsmart Yes, it is. But it's more useful to bring a phrase book.

2. **From:** nocreditcard ? (safe / carry cash)

   From: travelsmart

3. **From:** walksalot ? (good / rent a car)

   From: travelsmart

4. **From:** concernedtourist ? (easy / find good restaurants)

   From: travelsmart

5. **From:** nightowl ? (hard / get around at night)

   From: travelsmart

6. **From:** advanceplanner ? (necessary / make hotel reservations)

   From: travelsmart

Things to remember

1 What is it?

Vocabulary **A** Write the words under the pictures.

1. _____a tent_____

2. _____

3. _____

4. _____

5. _____

6. _____

B Circle the correct words, and complete the sentences.

1. You use __toothpaste__ with your toothbrush to clean your teeth.
   a. soap   b. a tent   ⓒ toothpaste

2. You use _____ at the beach if you don't want to get a sunburn.
   a. makeup   b. sunscreen   c. a pair of scissors

3. You wear _____ when you go to bed.
   a. pajamas   b. a bathing suit   c. sandals

4. Most people use _____ to wash their hair.
   a. soap   b. a brush   c. shampoo

5. When you go camping, you use _____ in your tent because you don't have a bed.
   a. insect repellent   b. a flashlight   c. a sleeping bag

6. A lot of men use _____ to remove the hair on their faces.
   a. a brush   b. a razor   c. a towel

7. If you are hurt or sick while camping, get medicine from _____ .
   a. batteries   b. a towel   c. a first-aid kit

8. Bring extra _____ with you to get power for your flashlight or radio.
   a. batteries   b. pajamas   c. makeup

9. Wear _____ to keep your feet cool when it's hot.
   a. sunglasses   b. sandals   c. a hat

10. People sometimes wear _____ on their faces to look good.
    a. sunscreen   b. makeup   c. insect repellent

2 I think you should . . .

Grammar **A** Complete the suggestions using the expressions in the box and your own ideas.

bring more than one credit card	✓take insect repellent
pack a lot of light clothes	use a lot of sunscreen

1. *A* We're going hiking in the mountains this weekend. What should we take?

   B Well, you should take insect repellent and a first-aid kit .

2. *A* I'm planning a skiing trip to British Columbia. The weather's nice there.

   B But it's easy to get a sunburn. You should _____ .

3. *A* I want to go to Hawaii on my next vacation.

   B You should _____ .

4. *A* My mother and I are planning a shopping trip to Hong Kong.

   B You really should _____ .

B Rewrite the suggestions in part A to make them softer.

1. I think you should take some insect repellent and a first-aid kit.

2. _____

3. _____

4. _____

3 Travel suggestions

Grammar and vocabulary Look at the brochures. Write three suggestions for people going on the trips.

White-water Rafting

Hike in Alaska!

Visit beautiful Bangkok

1. Don't forget to pack a bathing suit.

2. _____

3. _____

That's a great idea.

1 Responding to suggestions

Conversation strategies

Who really likes each suggestion? Circle the best response.

1. Let's go to Tsukiji for sushi tomorrow.
   - ⓐ That's a great idea.
   - b. I don't know. I don't really like fish.
2. We should go hiking together sometime.
   - a. I'd love to! When?
   - b. Maybe someday.
3. Why don't we get some tickets and see a show?
   - a. I don't know. Aren't tickets pretty expensive?
   - b. That sounds like fun. What do you want to see?
4. Would you like to go shopping for souvenirs this morning?
   - a. That sounds like a good idea. Where do you want to go?
   - b. Yeah, maybe we should do that sometime.
5. Let's drive through South America next summer.
   - a. I'd like to, but I need to get a part-time job.
   - b. That's an interesting idea. When do we leave?

2 That sounds great.

Conversation strategies

Use the cues to give two responses to these suggestions
(+ = you want to; – = you don't want to).

1. *A* Let's drive up to the mountains next weekend.

   B (+) _That sounds great. When should we leave?_

   (–) _I don't know. It's pretty cold this time of year._

2. *A* We could take a semester off from school and go backpacking.

   B (+) _____

   (–) _____

3. *A* Why don't we go to snorkeling sometime?

   B (+) _____

   (–) _____

4. *A* We should go camping in the outback next spring.

   B (+) _____

   (–) _____

5. *A* Why don't we just stay home, watch TV, and relax over the winter break?

   B (+) _____

   (–) _____

3 *I guess . . .*

Conversation strategies

Add *I guess* to these conversations. Check (✓) the correct blank.

1. *Maria*   Would you like to go dancing tomorrow night?
   Nick   _____ I have to work, but __✓__ I could go Sunday night.

2. *Lucy*   Why don't you come to Brazil with me next month? It would be fun.
   Emi   _____ I should get away. But I have exams then _____ .

3. *Tania*   I'm hungry. Let's try that new Mexican restaurant downtown.
   Sylvia   We could try it, _____ , but I really want some Italian food _____ .

4. *Olivia*   I went to India last summer, and the food was amazing! I loved it!
   Chad   Yeah, _____ it's good. _____ I could make some Indian food tonight.

5. *Marc*   Mandy and I have four tickets to a Broadway show on Friday.
         You and Mari should come with us.
   Taka   We could, _____ , but _____ we don't have a babysitter.

6. *Ming*   We should travel while we're still young.
   Jack   Yeah, _____ , but where would we go? We don't have any money _____ !

4 *Let's see a movie.*

Conversation strategies

Unscramble the suggestions. Write your own responses using *I guess*.
Add more information.

1. tonight / Let's / after class / see a movie .

   > Let's see a movie after class tonight.

   > I guess we could. I don't have any plans.

2. drive / Why / to the beach / don't we ?

3. grandmother / visit / this weekend / Let's / your .

4. don't we / in the mountains / go camping / Why ?

5. could / We / a couple of weeks / for / to Europe / go .

6. want to / meet / Do / my / you / parents ?

1 A trip of a lifetime

Reading **A** Read Joel's Web journal about his trip to Kenya. Then circle this information in the text.

| the animals he saw | the lakes he visited | the mountain where he hiked |

Joel's journal

JOEL'S **TRAVEL** PAGE

I just returned from an exciting tour of Kenya. It was the trip of a lifetime – there was so much to see!

My tour group spent the first two days at Masai Mara, driving around to see animals in their natural environment. We got close to elephants, cheetahs, and zebras, and we took some excellent photographs! On the third day, we went to Lake Naivasha. We stayed in little huts near the lake, where we could see local birds and hippos. I was surprised to find out that hippos kill more people than any other animal. That night we did some stargazing. The night was clear and perfect – I've never seen so many stars!

The next morning, we visited Lake Nakuru, where we saw a rare black rhino and hundreds of pink flamingos. That night, we camped in a place where we heard lions walking around near our campsite! Luckily, we never saw them, but we did not sleep very well. On day five, we took a trip to Thompson's Falls. It was hard to climb to the top, but it was worth the effort – the enormous waterfall was beautiful. We had a nice picnic lunch by the water.

Thompson's Falls

Masai dancers

The next day, we went to Mount Kenya, where we visited a Masai village. That night, we tried to do some traditional Masai dancing, and believe me, we looked very funny! We spent the seventh day hiking on Mount Kenya, and afterwards we made a trip to the local Kikuyu school. We talked to the students and teachers there and learned about their projects. Then we ate *irio* together, a traditional Kikuyu dish.

Back in Nairobi, Kenya's capital city, we had a tour of the city. Then we took our guides out to dinner to thank them for showing us their beautiful country.

The next morning, we made the long journey home. I was tired, but very sorry to leave. Visiting Kenya was my best vacation ever.

B Read the Web journal again. Write down two activities that Joel did at each place.

1. Masai Mara   *He drove around to see animals and took some photographs.*

2. Lake Naivasha _____

3. Lake Nakuru _____

4. Thompson's Falls _____

5. Mount Kenya _____

6. the Kikuyu school _____

7. Nairobi _____

2 A postcard from Ireland

Writing **A** Read Annie's postcard to Beth. Then match the postcard
sections to the correct sentences.

- Say something you are going to do.
- Describe the place, food, or weather.
- End with a closing.
- Start with a greeting.
- Say something you did.
- Say if you're enjoying your stay.

Dear Beth,

I'm having a fabulous time here in Ireland.

We are staying in Baltimore, a picturesque fishing village.

Today we went kayaking and saw birds and seals.

Tomorrow our guide will take us to some beautiful beaches and to an old castle. It's going to be a lot of fun.

See you next week!
Annie

Beth O'Hara
40 W. 20th St.
Apt. 6C
New York, NY 10011
U.S.A.

B Write a postcard to a friend about an imaginary visit to another place.

Dear

Unit 7 Progress chart

Mark the boxes below to rate your progress. ☑ = I know how to . . . [?] = I need to review how to . . .	To review, go back to these pages in the Student's Book.
Grammar	
☐ use infinitives to give reasons	66 and 67
☐ use *It's* + adjective + *to* . . .	66 and 67
☐ ask for and give advice and suggestions	69
Vocabulary	
☐ name at least 5 things to do to get ready for a trip	66 and 67
☐ name at least 12 things to pack for different kinds of trips	68 and 69
Conversation strategies	
☐ respond to suggestions I like and don't like	70 and 71
☐ use *I guess* when I'm unsure about something	71
Writing	
☐ format and use correct expressions in a postcard	73

Unit 8 At home

Spring cleaning

1 Whose is it?

Grammar and vocabulary

A Complete the chart with the correct pronouns.

Subject pronouns	Object pronouns	Possessive adjectives	Possessive pronouns
I	me		mine
you			
he			
she		her	
we			
they			

B Look at the pictures, and write questions with *Whose*. Then answer the questions using possessive pronouns.

1. *A* ___Whose suitcases are those?___
   B ___They're ours.___

2. *A* _____
   B _____

3. *A* _____
   B _____

4. *A* _____
   B _____

5. *A* _____
   B _____

6. *A* _____
   B _____

58

2 After the party

Grammar **Circle the correct words to complete the conversation.**

Karen Wow! What a mess.

Matt Are all of these things **our /** (**ours**)?

Karen No, they're things people forgot when they left the party last night.

Matt Well, I'm looking for **my / mine** jacket.

Karen Is this jacket **your / yours**?

Matt No, that's not **my / mine**. **My / mine** jacket is blue. I guess that's Felipe's.

Karen No, it's not **him / his**. Felipe's jacket is gray.

Matt Oh, well. Wow! Look at those DVDs. Whose are they?

Karen I think they're your parents'. Yeah, these are **their / theirs**. We borrowed them when we were at **their / theirs** house last weekend.

Matt Oh, yeah, . . . right. Hey, whose CDs are these? Are they Jan's?

Karen No, they're not **her / hers**. Can't you read? They say "Andy."

Matt No, I can't. I lost **my / mine** glasses, too!

Karen Wait a minute. Is this **your / yours** jacket?

Matt Yes, thanks! You're amazing. Now, do you think you can find **my / mine** glasses?

3 About you

Grammar and vocabulary **Are these sentences true or false for you? Write *T* (true) or *F* (false). Then correct the false sentences.**

1. I can never find anything in my closet. __F__

   I can usually find things in my closet but not in my drawers.

2. All of my CDs are in a box on top of my desk. _____

   _____

3. I put things like my I.D. card and passport in a drawer in my dresser. _____

   _____

4. There's a box on the floor under my bed with photos and letters in it. _____

   _____

5. I put all my old magazines and books on a shelf in the closet. _____

   _____

6. I keep stuff like shampoo, brushes, and my hair dryer in a drawer. _____

   _____

7. My shoes are on a small shelf on the floor of my closet. _____

   _____

1 Rooms and things

Vocabulary **A** There are 20 home items in the puzzle. Find the other 18. Look in these directions (→↓).

Q	A	R	M	C	H	A	I	R	Q	W	T	B	A
R	U	B	H	T	K	V	P	G	H	M	L	A	J
L	E	C	A	R	P	E	T	U	K	I	Y	T	K
E	K	F	S	S	A	L	Q	W	E	R	R	H	C
S	D	I	S	H	W	A	S	H	E	R	F	T	C
E	R	S	T	O	V	M	O	A	P	O	B	U	U
R	E	C	O	W	T	P	F	E	M	R	G	B	R
C	S	O	V	E	N	N	A	F	A	U	C	E	T
A	S	A	E	R	B	U	K	R	W	C	L	O	A
B	E	M	I	C	R	O	W	A	V	E	Z	A	I
I	R	Q	U	X	L	S	I	N	K	I	K	Z	N
N	M	N	I	G	H	T	S	T	A	N	D	E	S
E	S	E	C	U	S	H	I	O	N	S	R	X	Z
T	O	I	L	E	T	R	E	S	Y	L	V	A	D
S	F	A	C	O	F	F	E	E	T	A	B	L	E

B Read the clues and write the rooms in the center of the webs. Then complete the webs with words from part A. Some words can be used more than once.

1. I sleep in this room.

dresser

bedroom

2. I cook and sometimes eat in this room.

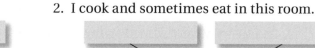

3. I wash my face and brush my teeth in this room.

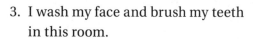

4. In this room, I listen to music, watch TV, and relax.

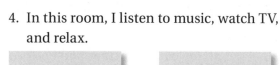

2 *I like that one.*

Grammar

Look at the pictures. Complete the questions with *one* or *ones*.
Then write answers using at least two adjectives.

1. **A** I like the Thai sofa. Which <u>one</u> do you like?
   B <u>Oh, I like the big Italian one.</u>

2. **A** I like the white dresser. Which _____ do you like?
   B _____

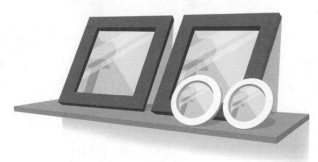

3. **A** I like the square mirrors. Which _____ do you like?
   B _____

4. **A** I love the big clock. Which _____ do you like?
   B _____

3 *Susan's living room*

Grammar and vocabulary

Unscramble the sentences about Susan's living room.

1. small / living room / There's / a / sofa / in / her / red
   <u>There's a small red sofa in her living room.</u>

2. has / square / some / cool / cushions / She / on the sofa
   _____

3. end table / a / There's / beautiful /on the left / Japanese
   _____

4. a / TV / She / big / on the wall / has / black
   _____

5. in front of / There's / a / the / coffee table / sofa / long / dark
   _____

6. are / on the floor / some / cotton / nice / rugs / There
   _____

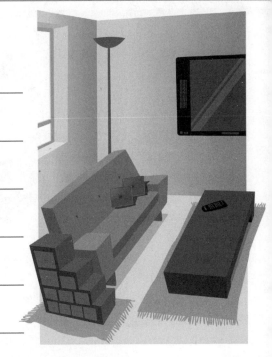

1 Asking politely

| Conversation strategies |

Complete the questions with *Would you mind* or *Do you mind if*.

1. *A* <u>Do you mind if</u> I borrow your dictionary?
   B No, not at all. Go ahead.

2. *A* _____ answering the phone for me?
   B Oh, no. No problem.

3. *A* _____ closing that door?
   B No, not at all.

4. *A* _____ I take off my shoes?
   B No. Go right ahead.

5. *A* _____ I use your computer for a minute?
   B No problem.

6. *A* _____ handing me the potato salad?
   B Of course not. Here you are.

7. *A* _____ playing that song again?
   B I'd be happy to.

8. *A* _____ I eat the last piece of apple pie?
   B Not at all. Go ahead.

9. *A* _____ I turn on the news for a minute?
   B No, not at all.

10. *A* _____ turning down the music a little?
    B No problem. Is this OK now?

2 *No problem.*

Circle the correct responses to complete the conversation.

Mother Rudy, can I talk to you?

Rudy (Sure.) / **No, not at all.** You don't sound too happy, Mom. What's the matter?

Mother It's your room. It's a mess. Could you please clean it before your grandparents get here?

Rudy **Oh, no. / OK.** I can do it now.

Mother Oh, and would you mind taking your weight-training things out of the living room?

Rudy **No, go right ahead. / No, not at all.** But do you mind if I do it after I clean my room?

Mother **No, of course not. / Sure, I'd be happy to.** Actually, I should probably call your grandparents to make sure they're not lost. Do you know their cell-phone number?

Rudy Yeah, I've got it on my phone.

Mother Oh, in that case, can I borrow your phone?

Rudy **Oh, no. No problem. / Sure, go ahead.**

Mother Where is it?

Rudy Uh . . . I don't know. I think it's here somewhere. . . .

3 *Requests, requests*

Respond to these requests. Add more information.

1. *A* I don't usually stay up this late. Would you mind bringing me some coffee?
   B No, of course not. But I have to make some first.

2. *A* Do you mind if I come over to your house tonight? I want to watch the soccer game.
   B _____

3. *A* These tacos are really spicy. Could you get me a glass of water?
   B _____

4. *A* Can I borrow your phone? I'd like to call my friend in Australia.
   B _____

5. *A* Sorry, I can't hear you. Would you mind turning down the music a little?
   B _____

6. *A* Is it dark in here, or is it me? Do you mind if I turn on the lamp?
   B _____

7. *A* Boy, I'm starving. Can you make me something to eat?
   B _____

8. *A* Could I borrow your silver necklace? I have a big date tonight.
   B _____

Home habits

1 Cat habitat

Reading **A** **What do you think these words mean?**

| houseboat | cat boat | stray cat | cat lady |

B **Read the article and check the meaning of the words in part A.**

All aboard, furry neighbors!

Have you ever lived next door to a boat? How about a boat full of cats?

Amsterdam, the largest city in the Netherlands, is full of canals. There are many different kinds of boats on the canals. Some of them carry people and goods, some have shops or restaurants on them, while others are houseboats – boats that people live on. But not only people live on these houseboats. Cats do too, at least on two of them.

It all began in 1966 with a stray cat, her kittens, and a kind woman named Henriette van Weelde. One rainy night, Henriette heard a cat crying outside her house. She opened the door and saw a wet mother cat trying to protect her kittens from the rain. Henriette felt sorry for the poor animals, so she let them live with her. Soon another stray cat joined them, and then more. Henriette quickly became known as the "cat lady."

Before long, the cats filled Henriette's house. Then they filled her garden. And the cats kept coming. What could she do with them all? She saw the answer to her problem floating on the canal – a houseboat. People could live on houseboats, so why couldn't cats? In 1968, Henriette bought her first "cat boat."

Soon, even more stray cats moved in, and then came people who wanted to help – the first volunteers. But after just three years, the houseboat was full of cats. So Henriette bought another boat! More people were visiting, not just to bring cats in, but also to adopt a pet or just to look. After all, a houseboat for cats is not a common sight!

Today, Henriette's two cat boats are still in the same place on the canal. And the Cat Boat Foundation that Henriette started years ago is not only an official Dutch charity but also an international tourist attraction!

C **Read these questions. Find the answers in the article.**

1. What are boats used for on Amsterdam's canals? _They're used to carry people and goods, for restaurants and shops, and to live on._

2. Why did Henriette van Weelde take in the first stray cat? _____

_____

3. What did Henriette do when her house and garden filled with cats? _____

_____

4. Who helped Henriette take care of the cats? _____

_____

5. What are two reasons people visit Henriette's cat boats? _____

_____

2 A typical Sunday

A Read the statements. Choose the correct words to complete the sentences.

1. __First__ , Danny wakes up around noon on Sunday. (first / as soon as)
2. He sleeps for thirty or so minutes more _____ he gets out of bed. (before / after)
3. _____ , he takes a quick shower, gets dressed, and goes downstairs. (then / while)
4. _____ , he goes into the kitchen and makes a huge breakfast. (when / next)
5. _____ he's eating breakfast, he reads the sports section of the paper. (during / while)
6. He checks his e-mail messages _____ he finishes his breakfast. (when / next)
7. He watches football on TV _____ he's off the computer. (as soon as / then)
8. He usually falls asleep once or twice _____ the game. (during / while)
9. _____ the game is over, Danny goes upstairs and takes a long nap. (then / after)

B Write true sentences about your Sunday afternoons. Use *first, next, then, before, after, during, as soon as, while,* and *when.*

```
1. First, I
2.
3.
4.
5.
6.
7.
8.
9.
```

Unit 8 Progress chart

Mark the boxes below to rate your progress. ☑ = I know how to . . . ? = I need to review how to . . .	To review, go back to these pages in the Student's Book.
Grammar	
☐ ask questions with *Whose*	76 and 77
☐ use possessive pronouns	76 and 77
☐ order adjectives before nouns and before the pronouns *one* and *ones*	79
☐ use location expressions after nouns and pronouns	79
Vocabulary	
☐ name at least 6 places to keep things in my home	75
☐ name at least 15 home items for different rooms	78
Conversation strategies	
☐ request permission politely to do things with *Do you mind if . . . ?*	80 and 81
☐ make requests politely with *Would you mind . . . ?*	80 and 81
☐ agree to requests in different ways	81
Writing	
☐ order events using sequencing words	83

Unit 9 Things happen

When things go wrong . . .

1 What were they doing?

Grammar Circle the correct verb forms in these stories.

1. A friend and I **ran / were running** in the park, and these guys **rode / were riding** their bikes behind us. We didn't hear them because we **listened / were listening** to music. Anyway, we **decided / were deciding** to stop because I was tired, and one of the guys **bumped / was bumping** right into me. And then they just **rode / were riding** away!

2. An embarrassing thing **happened / was happening** when I **studied / was studying** singing at the university. At my first concert, when I **walked / was walking** to the stage, I **saw / was seeing** a concert hall full of people. I **got / was getting** so scared that I completely **forgot / was forgetting** the words and then the music to my song. So I just **stood / was standing** on the stage, and then I **said / was saying**, "Thank you." After that, I **walked / was walking** off and **went / was going** home.

2 Interruptions

Grammar Complete the sentences with the correct form of the verbs in the box.

✓do	eat	go	run	spill	tell
delete	get	✓ring	send	talk	try

1. I __was doing__ the laundry when the phone __rang__ .
2. Chris _____ a joke when Maria _____ to the party.
3. Jeff accidentally _____ all of Yuri's files when he _____ to fix her computer.
4. Ryan and I _____ lunch when our server _____ coffee all over us.
5. Ming and Wei _____ home to Beijing, but the airline _____ their suitcases to Paris.
6. Trish _____ on her cell phone, and she _____ right into me.

3 Telling anecdotes

Grammar and vocabulary

Look at the pictures. Write sentences using the past continuous and the simple past.

1. A guy was having his lunch in the park. He was reading _____

_____

_____

_____

2. _____

_____

_____

_____

4 About you

Grammar

Complete the sentences with true information.

1. I was going to school last week when I saw our teacher in a bright red sports car .
2. When a friend of mine called the other day, _____ .
3. Last week, I was eating dinner and _____ .
4. I was talking to some friends once when _____ .
5. When the teacher walked into the classroom the other day, _____ .
6. I was trying to look cool once _____ .

Accidents happen.

1 Parts of the body

Vocabulary **A** Look at the pictures, and complete the puzzle.

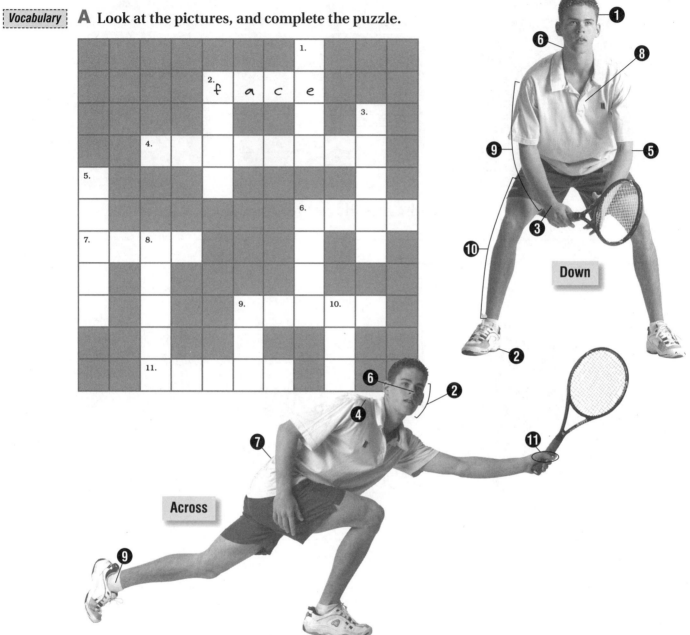

2. f a c e

Down

Across

B Circle the correct words, and complete the sentences.

1. I can't move. I hurt my __back__ .
   a. thumb   (b.) back   c. arm
2. It's hard to walk. I broke my _____ .
   a. nose   b. leg   c. shoulder
3. I cut my _____ . It hurts to smile.
   a. finger   b. toe   c. face
4. I sprained my _____ , so it's hard to write.
   a. wrist   b. ankle   c. chest
5. It hurts to wear high heels. I broke my _____ .
   a. finger   b. shoulder   c. toe

6. I got a black _____ . I can't see clearly.
   a. eye   b. head   c. neck
7. I can't bend my arm. I hurt my _____ .
   a. elbow   b. hip   c. knee
8. It's hard to wash dishes. I cut my _____ .
   a. knee   b. foot   c. hand
9. I hurt my _____ . I can't turn my head.
   a. thumb   b. neck   c. wrist
10. I broke my _____ . It's hard to breathe.
    a. nose   b. hip   c. eye

2 How did you hurt yourself?

Grammar Look at the pictures and the answers. Write the questions.

1. A <u>How did she hurt herself?</u>
   B When she was making tea, she burned her hand.

2. A _____
   B When we were running, I fell and sprained my ankle.

3. A _____
   B They hurt their backs when they were lifting some heavy boxes.

4. A _____
   B He was chopping vegetables for dinner when he cut his finger.

3 A wonderful day

Grammar Complete the conversation. Write the questions using the past continuous.

Mom Hi, honey. How was your day?

Alicia Well, I hurt myself. A ball I kicked hit me in the head.

Mom Oh, no! <u>What were you doing?</u>
 (What)

Alicia Well, I was playing soccer with some friends. I was looking in the other direction.

Mom _____
 (Why)

Alicia Well, I was looking at a guy. I guess I wasn't paying attention.

Mom _____
 (Who)

Alicia This really cute guy named Jason.

Mom _____
 (Was)

Alicia No, he wasn't playing with us. He was just standing there.

Mom _____
 (Where)

Alicia In front of the field. He was talking on the phone. Anyway, I kicked the ball, the ball hit Jason, and then it hit me.

Mom That's terrible!

Alicia Not really. Now I have a date him with on Saturday!

That's really funny!

1 I bet you felt bad!

Conversation strategies

Number the lines of the conversations in the correct order.

1. _____ Australia? That sounds like a fun trip.

   __1__ You won't believe what I did last week. I was riding my bike with a friend in City Park.

   _____ Yeah – there's more. I wasn't paying attention and ran right into a woman in front of me.

   _____ Yeah, it is. Anyway, my friend and I were talking about going to Australia.

   _____ Oh, that's a beautiful park.

   _____ I bet she wasn't too happy!

2. _____ Yeah. So I jumped out of bed, got dressed, and ran all the way to school.

   _____ You're kidding! That late?

   _____ I bet no one even noticed.

   _____ Yeah, I was. And when I got to class, I saw that I was wearing different sneakers!

   _____ Guess what I did? I woke up late this morning, and it was after 10:30.

   _____ The whole way? I bet you were exhausted!

3. _____ I know. The horse fell right on top of her, and she couldn't get up. But my father was nearby.

   _____ Yeah, it was. My dad took her to the hospital, and she's OK now.

   _____ Do you remember my cousin, Courtney? Well, one day last summer she was riding her horse when the horse fell.

   _____ That was lucky!

   _____ Oh, my gosh! That's awful.

   _____ I bet you're happy about that.

2 *I bet . . .*

Complete each conversation with an appropriate response using *I bet*.

1. *A* I was looking around in the mall the other day, and I walked right into a glass door! I was so embarrassed.

   B I bet no one even noticed.

2. *A* My sister wasn't paying attention when she was getting her newspaper this morning, and she locked herself out of her apartment.

   B _____

3. *A* My little sister borrowed my new laptop last night, and she dropped it! Can you believe it? It's broken.

   B _____

4. *A* I went to a concert with some friends last weekend, but I was so bored that I fell asleep!

   B _____

5. *A* Yesterday, I was singing loudly in the car. I forgot that the back windows were open. Everyone on the street heard me.

   B _____

6. *A* Guess what? I just won a trip to Hawaii in a radio contest!

   B _____

3 *And then what happened?*

Finish these anecdotes. Then write an appropriate response.

1. *A* I was walking to work one morning, and I thought I saw my old friend from junior high school across the street. I ran after him and called his name. When I got there, and saw the guy's face, I knew he wasn't my friend. I didn't know this guy at all.

   B Oh, no! I bet you were embarrassed.

2. *A* I was taking a taxi once, and I was in a hurry. I wanted to pay the driver with some cash from my wallet but _____

   _____

   B _____

3. *A* Last year, I thought everyone had forgotten my birthday. Well, when I got home, I opened the door and _____

   _____

   B _____

4. *A* My brother was driving my dad's car in a bad storm one night and _____

   _____

   B _____

1 What was it?

Reading **A** Read the story. Then circle the best title.

Strange Lights
An Unusual Server
The Dangers of Fog

A few years ago, while I was driving across eastern Canada, something very unusual happened. I still don't understand what happened.

While I was driving at night through thick, heavy fog, I noticed flashes of light in the sky. They were moving from the sky onto the road in front of my truck. I was driving slowly, and I couldn't see very well, but those lights were as bright as daylight, and they were blue. It was definitely not lightning.

Now here's where the story gets weird. I was getting tired of driving in the fog, so I pulled off the road and stopped at an all-night restaurant for travelers.

I walked in and sat down at the counter. When the server came to my table, she laughed and asked me how I got such a bad sunburn. I didn't know what she meant, but my face suddenly felt really hot. I went into the restroom and looked at myself in the mirror. My face was bright red! I splashed cold water on it and held a towel to my skin. My hands were also burned. I was very puzzled and a little frightened.

I went back to my table and ordered something to eat. I was feeling weak and extremely tired, and I wasn't hungry anymore. After I forced myself to eat a few bites of food, I checked into a nearby motel, where I slept for about 24 hours. After that, I didn't see any more light flashes, and the "sunburn" on my face and hands disappeared after a few days. Even now, I wonder about those flashes of light — I'll never forget them!

B Read the story again. Write *T* (true) or *F* (false) for each sentence. Then correct the false sentences.

1. The unusual event happened a few ~~months~~ *years* ago. __F__

2. The man saw the flashes of light while he was driving one foggy night. _____

3. He noticed his sunburn before he went into the restaurant. _____

4. The server was frightened by the man's appearance. _____

5. The man ate a big meal at the restaurant because he wasn't hungry. _____

6. After the man checked into a motel, he slept for a long time. _____

7. The man didn't see any more light flashes after that night. _____

8. The burns disappeared on his face after a few years. _____

2 Two unusual events

Writing **A** Read about two unusual events. Complete the stories using *when* or *while*.

❶ Years ago, **when** my friend and I were in junior high school, we decided to write our names on a one-dollar bill for fun. We spent the money and forgot about it. Then, one night about 20 years later _____ I was waiting for a bus, I saw a dollar bill on the street. I picked it up, and my name was on it. It was the same bill we wrote on! _____ I think of it now, I'm amazed!

– *Ken Leonard, Los Angeles*

❷ I had a strange experience a couple of months ago. It happened one night _____ I was sleeping. It was probably about two in the morning _____ I woke up to loud music. _____ I looked around, I saw that the CD player on my computer was running. I clearly remember turning it off _____ I went to bed.

– *Lisa Lee, Hong Kong*

B Write about an unusual event that happened to you or to someone you know.

A really unusual thing happened to

Unit 9 Progress chart

Mark the boxes below to rate your progress. ✓ = I know how to . . . ？ = I need to review how to . . .	To review, go back to these pages in the Student's Book.
Grammar	
☐ make past continuous statements	86 and 87
☐ ask past continuous questions	89
☐ use reflexive pronouns	89
Vocabulary	
☐ name at least 12 parts of the body	88
☐ name at least 6 injuries	88 and 89
Conversation strategies	
☐ react to and comment on a story	90 and 91
☐ respond with *I bet*	91
Writing	
☐ link ideas with *when* and *while*	93

Unit 10 Communication

Keeping in touch

1 Bigger and better

Grammar **A** Complete the chart below with the comparative form of the adjectives in the box.

bad	cheap	easy	hard	noisy	quick
✓big	convenient	expensive	important	old	slow
boring	cool	fun	interesting	personal	small
busy	difficult	good	new	popular	useful

Adjective + -er / -ier		more / less + adjective		Irregular adjectives	
bigger					

B Complete the sentences with the comparative form of the adjectives.

1. Postcards are __slower__ (slow) than e-mail.
2. Cell-phone service is _____ (expensive) than regular phone service.
3. Instant messaging is _____ (easy) than text messaging.
4. I think e-cards are _____ (convenient) than regular cards.
5. To me, regular photos are _____ (nice) than digital photos.
6. I think junk mail is even _____ (bad) than spam.
7. It's _____ (important) to have a phone than to have a computer.
8. Online newspapers are _____ (good) than regular newspapers.

C Complete the conversation.

Dong Un I love my new laptop. It's so much _____ (good) than my old desktop.

Loni But aren't regular computers _____ (cheap) than laptops?

Dong Un Yes, but they're _____ (useful) than laptops because you can't take them to the library or on a trip.

Loni Well, maybe laptops are _____ (cool) than desktops, but my big computer is _____ (quick) than most laptops.

Dong Un Yeah, but it sure is a lot _____ (heavy)!

2 Desktops are less convenient . . .

Grammar Look at the pictures. Correct the sentences to match the pictures.

1. Jason thinks desktop computers are more convenient than laptops.

   Jason thinks desktop computers are
   less convenient than laptops.

2. Sandra thinks e-cards are more fun than postcards.

   _____

   _____

3. Robert's grandparents think instant messaging is easier than phone calls.

   _____

   _____

4. Jay and Sun Hee think video conferences are more boring than long business meetings.

   _____

   _____

3 I don't think so!

Grammar and vocabulary Disagree with the statements.

1. *A* I think VCRs are harder to use than DVD players.

   B _Really? I think VCRs are easier to use than DVD players._

2. *A* To me, regular cameras take better pictures than cell-phone cameras.

   B _____

3. *A* I think radios are noisier than CD players.

   B _____

4. *A* It's easier to understand a voice-mail message than a written one.

   B _____

5. *A* It's hard when your cell phone doesn't work, but it's worse when your computer is broken.

   B _____

6. *A* In my opinion, text messages are more popular than phone calls to keep in touch.

   B _____

1 Phone situations

Vocabulary **A** **Choose the correct word to complete each phone expression.**

1. have a bad ___b___   a. message   b. connection   c. number
2. call me _____   a. number   b. connection   c. back
3. have another _____   a. call   b. number   c. mistake
4. leave a _____   a. back   b. message   c. call
5. have the wrong _____   a. number   b. mistake   c. connection
6. please hold _____   a. on   b. in   c. call
7. get cut _____   a. back   b. on   c. off

B **Use the phone expressions in part A to complete the sentences.**

1. Sheila called me at work, but I was in an important meeting and couldn't talk. I asked Sheila to ___call me back___ later.

2. Rick can't hear Andrea because there's too much noise on the line. They _____ .

3. William needs to talk to Jessica, but she's not home. He wants her to return his call, so he'll have to _____ .

4. Jim wanted to call his brother, but he accidentally called someone he didn't know. He _____ .

5. I have problems with my cell phone. Every time I walk into my bedroom, I hear a tone and then I _____ .

6. I called Mike, but his wife said he was upstairs watching TV. She asked me to _____ while she called him to the phone.

7. Jeri works at home, and she gets a lot of phone calls. Every time I call her, I have to hold on because she _____ .

2 How do they respond?

Grammar
and
vocabulary

Circle the best response for each phone expression.

1. I can't hear you. We have a bad connection.
   a. I have another call.
   (b.) Call me back on a different phone.

2. Please leave a message.
   a. Hi, Frank. This is Manny. Call me at home.
   b. Frank is on the phone.

3. Can you hold on, please?
   a. Sure, no problem.
   b. I got cut off.

4. Oh, I'm sorry. I think I have the wrong number.
   a. One moment, please.
   b. No problem.

5. Good morning, Cambridge University Press.
   a. Would you like to leave a message?
   b. Could I speak to Sally Smith, please?

6. Did you get my message?
   a. Yeah, I think I did.
   b. No problem.

3 More than you!

Grammar

Complete the sentences with *more*, *less*, or *fewer*.

1. *Nancy* Wow! Look at my mailbox. It's full. I get __more__ junk mail than you do.

   Bill Yeah, but you only had two spam messages last week. I had twenty!
   I get _____ spam than you do.

2. *Julie* Oh, no! My cell-phone bill is really high this month! I need to talk _____ than
   I did last month.

   Paula Let me see. Sixty dollars? That's not bad. Mine was ninety-five dollars.
   My cell phone costs me _____ money than yours!

3. *Dan* I only had two text messages last month. I get _____ text messages than phone calls.

   Eric I don't really like to use my cell phone too much. Actually, I like instant messaging
   _____ than text messaging.

4. *Miki* Would you turn that computer off? You spend _____ time online than anyone I know!

   Larry Well, I'm bored. You're always watching TV. You could watch _____ TV, you know!

5. *Ben* Oh, no! The server is down *again*! I need to change my provider to yours. You seem to
   have a lot _____ problems with your Internet service provider than I do.

   Paul I don't know. My provider breaks down _____ than your provider, but your service
   has _____ useful features than mine has.

What were you saying?

1 Exciting news

Conversation strategies

A Complete the chart below with expressions from the phone conversation.

Ellen Tommy? It's Ellen. You won't believe it!

Tommy Sorry, Ellen. Can you hold on a minute? I have to turn the radio down. . . . OK, what were you saying?

Ellen Remember that job interview I had last week?

Tommy Sure, I do. Oh, just a second. My cell phone's ringing. . . . So, where were we?

Ellen My job interview last week. They called this morning and – oops! Excuse me just a minute. I spilled my tea. . . . What was I saying?

Tommy They called about the job. . . .

Ellen Yeah, right. I got the job! I start next month.

Tommy Next month? That's great! Oh, just a minute. I need to switch phones. . . . OK, so you were saying?

Ellen This is the exciting part! Can you wait just a second? I need to turn off the stove. . . . All right. Where was I?

Tommy The exciting part about your new job.

Ellen Right! They want me to work in their London office!

Tommy That's amazing! Congratulations, Ellen!

Interrupting a conversation	Restarting a conversation
1. Can you hold on a minute?	1. OK, what were you saying?
2.	2.
3.	3.
4.	4.
5.	5.

B Complete the conversations with expressions from the chart in part A.

1. *Nolan* Hi, Akemi! I have some good news.
   Akemi Oh, I'm sorry. _____ I have another call.
   Nolan Sure, I don't mind.

2. *Abby* Kyle, it's Abby. I'm at the supermarket and . . .
   Kyle Just a second. I have to turn off the TV. _____
   Abby I was saying, I'm at the supermarket. Can you come pick me up?

3. *Muriel* Hey, it's me. I'm calling because I'm – oops! Hold on, I dropped my briefcase. . . . _____
   Brett You're calling because you're . . .
   Muriel Oh, yes, I'm working late. I'll be home around nine tonight.

2 I just need to . . .

Conversation
strategies
Add *just* to the sentences to make them softer.

1. I need to ask you a few questions. <u>I just need to ask you a few questions.</u>

2. Sure. Can you wait a minute? _____

3. I have to answer the door. _____

4. Could you hold on a second? _____

5. I need to turn off the faucet. _____

6. I want to answer a call on another line. _____

7. I'm calling to find out about your test. _____

8. I have to tell you one thing. _____

3 Hold on a second.

Conversation
strategies
**Imagine your friend John calls. Follow the instructions and complete the
conversation. Use *just* where possible.**

You Hello?

John Hi, It's John! How are you doing?

You <u>Hey, John! I'm fine. Can you hold on a second? I just want to turn down the music.</u>
  <u>So, what were you saying?</u>
  (Respond. / Interrupt to turn down the music. / Restart the conversation.)

John I was just calling to ask about your English class. How's it going?

You _____

  _____
  (Talk about your English class. / Interrupt because there's noise on the line. / Switch phones. / Restart the conversation.)

John You like your English class. Hey, guess what! I started a Spanish class last week. It's a lot
  of fun, and I'm really learning a lot.

You _____

  _____
  (Respond. / Interrupt to close the window. / Restart the conversation.)

John My Spanish class. Well, anyway, do you have any plans for this weekend?

You _____

  _____
  (Talk about your plans. / Interrupt to answer the door. / Restart the conversation.)

John I just wanted to see if you'd like to see a movie or something Saturday night.

You _____

  _____
  (Accept the invitation. / Ask if you can call him back later because your apple pie is burning.)

John Sure, no problem. Talk to you later.

You _____

  _____
  (Thank him for calling. / Say good-bye.)

1 What's a blog?

Reading **A** **What do you think a *blog* is? Check (✓) your guess. Then read the article.**

☐ a computer support Web site ☐ a weather information Web site ☐ an online diary about a particular topic

---

Web Logs

BLOGGING

Do you have a blog? Do you know someone who does? Chances are you do. Blogging is one of the most popular forms of modern publishing.

A Web log – or "blog," for short – is a kind of online diary that features one person's ideas and opinions. The entries are updated regularly, and they can be from a few sentences to several paragraphs long. Blogs are usually about one main topic, such as politics, sports, or entertainment. The site often has links to other interesting Web sites, as well as a place for readers to post their own comments and feedback.

The first blogs were created in the 1990s to list the interesting sites people found on the Internet and comment on them. There weren't many blogs because a computer expert had to create them. However, this changed in 1999, when free blog-building software first became available. Suddenly, it was easy to start a site. Between 2000 and 2001, the number of blogs increased more than 600%. In 2005, there were more than 5 million blogs.

What kind of person has a blog? Interestingly, more women than men have active blogs on the Internet. Less than half of all bloggers are men. In addition, typical bloggers are young. More than 90% of bloggers are under 30 years old. In fact, the average blogger is a teenage girl who updates her site every two weeks just to keep in touch with her friends about her life.

People write blogs for other reasons, too. The Internet contains a lot of information, and it can be very helpful to find out which sites have more information than others. Many bloggers are people who want to share information about useful Web sites. Other bloggers are writers who want people around the world to read their personal ideas and opinions. People can publish their writing more quickly on a blog than in a book or magazine. Moreover, they are their own editor – they can publish whatever and whenever they want.

Blogging is one of the fastest-growing forms of publishing, and because every blogger can have instant readers, blogging is probably here to stay!

B **Read the text again, and answer the questions.**

1. When and why did the first blogs appear? *The first blogs appeared in the 1990s to share information about interesting Web sites.*

2. Why was there such a big increase in blogs after 1999? _____

3. Who is the average blogger? What does this person write about? _____

4. What are two reasons that people write blogs? _____

2 Pros and cons

Writing **A** Read the article. Then match each section to the correct paragraph.

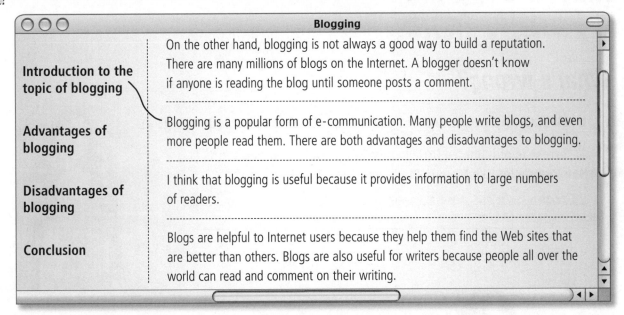

B Write a short article on a form of e-communication. Include an introduction, the advantages, the disadvantages, and a conclusion giving your opinion.

> is very popular these days.

Unit 10 Progress chart

Mark the boxes below to rate your progress. ☑ = I know how to . . . ? = I need to review how to . . .	To review, go back to these pages in the Student's Book.
Grammar ☐ make comparisons with adjectives ☐ use *more*, *less*, and *fewer* with nouns and verbs	98 and 99 101
Vocabulary ☐ name at least 6 kinds of electronic communication ☐ use at least 5 different phone expressions	97 and 98 100 and 101
Conversation strategies ☐ interrupt and restart conversations on the phone ☐ use *just* to soften things I say	102 and 103 103
Writing ☐ write an article including the advantages and disadvantages of a topic and a conclusion with my views	105

Unit **11** Appearances

Family traits

1 What's wrong?

Grammar
and
vocabulary

Look at the pictures. Correct the three mistakes in each description.

1. Teresa is old. She's a little heavy. She's got long blond hair. She looks a lot like Megan. She's wearing a black sweater.

   Teresa isn't old. She's young.

   _____

   _____

2. Megan is young. She's very thin with long curly hair. She looks a lot like Teresa. She's wearing a white sweater.

   _____

   _____

   _____

2 Do you look alike?

Grammar

Complete the conversation with the missing questions.

Kari Did you meet my brother Bob at the party last night? He's home for spring break.

David Do you look alike? _____

Kari No, we look totally different.

David _____ ?

Kari Actually, he takes after my mom. I look like my dad, I guess.

David _____ ?

Kari He's six four. He's a lot taller than me.

David _____ ?

Kari No, he doesn't. It's very curly. But it's blond like mine.

David _____ ?

Kari He's got green eyes.

David _____ ?

Kari He's twenty-one. Hey, there's Bob now! Let's go say hi!

3 A family portrait

Look at the picture, and answer the questions.

1. Who does Karen take after, Sharon or Dick?   <u>She takes after Sharon.</u>
2. Who's got dark hair? _____
3. Who's got straight hair? _____
4. Do Kevin and Joey look alike? _____
5. Who do Kevin and Joey take after? _____
6. Who's bald? _____

4 About you

Answer the questions with true information.

1. Are you taller or shorter than your parents?
   <u>I'm taller than my mother, but I'm shorter than my father.</u>

2. Who does your father take after, his mother or his father? How?

   _____

3. Do you look more like your father or your mother? How?

   _____

4. How many people have dark hair in your family?

   _____

5. What famous person do you look like? In what way do you look alike?

   _____

1 What is it?

A Read the clues and write the features.

1. These can make a person's teeth straight.   __braces__

2. This grows on a man's chin. _____

3. These are tiny braids close to a person's head. _____

4. People wear these to help them see better. _____

5. These have tiny holes for wearing jewelry. _____

6. People who do weight training usually get this way. _____

7. These are little brown spots on a person's face or body. _____

8. This grows under a man's nose. _____

9. This is what we call people with a shaved head. _____

10. Some women think these make their hands look pretty, and they sometimes paint them red. _____

11. People with long hair often wear it in one of these to keep their hair out of the way. _____

12. Young people sometimes like this style where the hair is short and stands up. _____

B Answer the questions with your own ideas and information.

1. Do you think men should have pierced ears? _No, I don't. I don't think men should wear jewelry._
   or _I think it's OK. Men wear rings and bracelets, so it's OK to wear earrings, too._

2. Who did you know with freckles when you were young? _____
   _____

3. Did you ever wear braces on your teeth? _____
   _____

4. Which is better, being muscular or being thin? Why? _____
   _____

5. What are your two favorite ways to wear long hair? _____
   _____

6. Who do you know with a shaved head? _____
   _____

2 Which one?

Grammar and vocabulary

Look at the picture. Write a sentence about each student using the given word and one other descriptive phrase.

1. *A* Which one is Lisa? (check)

   B Lisa is the one in the black jeans checking her grades.

2. *A* Which one is Julio? (stand)

   B _____

3. *A* Which one is Mei-ling? (listen)

   B _____

4. *A* Who is Luigi? (write)

   B _____

5. *A* What about Ivy, which one is she? (sit)

   B _____

6. *A* So which guy is Kareem? (wear)

   B _____

7. *A* Which one is Anna? (talk)

   B _____

8. *A* Is Kazu here? Who is he? (read)

   B _____

What's his name?

1 I can't remember.

Complete the conversations with the questions in the box.

What's his / her name?
What do you call it / them?
What do you call that thing / those things?

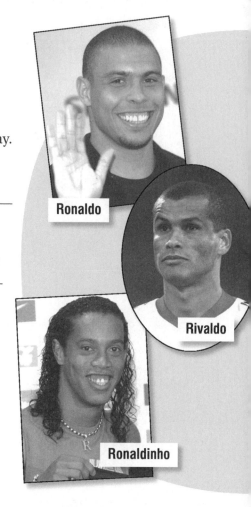

1. *Katherine* Hey, I got tickets to the big soccer match on Sunday.
   Yong Joon Cool. Who's playing?
   Katherine Well, it's an all-star match. That really famous
   Brazilian star is in it. <u>What's his name?</u>
   Yong Joon Do you mean Ronaldo?
   Katherine Maybe. What does he look like?
   Yong Joon He's got a bald head. . . . Well, not bald exactly. He
   cuts all his hair off. _____
   Katherine A shaved head. No, that's not him.
   Yong Joon Maybe you're thinking of Rivaldo.
   Katherine I'm not sure. The player I like the most has
   long hair, and he wears it in those long twisted
   things. _____
   Yong Joon Oh, I know who you mean – Ronaldinho.
   They're called dreadlocks. But he doesn't look
   like that anymore.
   Katherine Ronaldo, Rivaldo, Ronaldinho – no wonder I
   can never remember his name!

   Ronaldo

   Rivaldo

   Ronaldinho

2. *Brittany* Guess who I just saw at the airport! That singer, the
   one with the great voice.
   _____
   Ashley Sorry, that could be a lot of people. Can you give me
   more information?
   Brittany You know, she plays the piano and writes her own
   songs.
   Ashley Norah Jones?
   Brittany No, not her. This singer sometimes wears her hair in
   those little braids. _____
   Ashley Do you mean cornrows?
   Brittany Yeah, right. And sometimes she wears an earring that
   looks like a, um . . . _____
   Ashley I don't know what you call it. Anyway, you're talking
   about Alicia Keys, right?

Alicia Keys

2 Oh, you mean . . .

Who are they talking about? Respond using *You mean . . .* or *Do you mean . . . ?*
Then match the pictures.

1. *A* Who is that Mexican actress – the one who played
   Frida Kahlo in that movie?

   B Oh, you mean Salma Hayek.   d

2. *A* I really like those tennis players . . . what are their
   names? They're sisters with the cool tennis outfits.

   B _____ _____

3. *A* Do you want to go see that hip-hop band? You know, the
   one with the female lead singer?

   B _____ _____

4. *A* My friend just loves that Chinese basketball player. You
   know – the really tall one.

   B _____ _____

5. *A* I'm crazy about that actor – what's his name? – the really
   good-looking guy in *Pirates of the Caribbean*.

   B _____ _____

a Yao Ming
b Black Eyed Peas
c Johnny Depp
d Salma Hayek
e Venus and Serena Williams

3 Describe it.

Look at the pictures. Complete the descriptions without using the actual word(s).
Then respond with *You mean . . .* or *Do you mean . . . ?*

1. *A* My sister loves to wear those shoes that make women look really tall .
   B Do you mean high heels?

2. *A* My brother has that hair _____ .
   B _____

3. *A* I just bought some of those pants _____ .
   B _____

4. *A* My father has _____ .
   B _____

How we looked

1 Image makeovers

Reading **A** Look at the pictures. Match each picture with a year. Then read the article, and check your answers.

1985   1990   1995   1996   2000

Image overhaul, again and again

Party girl, glamorous movie star, or conservative mother of two? Madonna's image has changed more times than we can count. Throughout her long career, she has managed to stay ahead of everyone else and set new style trends every step of the way.

When she first started out as a club singer, she was wearing funky lace dresses, black rubber bracelets, and lots of necklaces. By 1985, she was so popular that many young girls were copying her look. The news media began to call these girls "Madonna Wannabes," or girls who "want to be" like Madonna.

In 1987, the singer began her "Who's That Girl?" world tour. The new album and music videos showed a radical transformation for the former party girl. She cut her long hair and dyed it blond, as she took on a more classic look.

Madonna continued to change her image as she began to appear in movies. For the film *Dick Tracy* in 1990, she became a glamorous blond movie star. In 1995, she even changed the color of her eyes to brown for the film *Evita*.

After the birth of her first child, Lourdes, in 1996, Madonna had another makeover, taking on the new image of a mother. Then Madonna married British film director Guy Ritchie and had her second child, Rocco, in 2000. During her "Drowned World" tour, her husband and children traveled with her, and the changes in Madonna's lifestyle, as well as her appearance, became clear to everyone. She no longer went to parties after concerts but went straight back to her hotel to spend time with her children. Gone was the wild girl of her early career. She was now someone who placed family first. She once said, "Love is more important than fame, money, and being with beautiful people."

After more than twenty years of singing and acting, Madonna is still one of the world's most popular stars. Her fans are always amazed at how she can make so many changes and never go out of style.

B Read the article again. Then correct these sentences.

1. Madonna started out as a ~~country~~ ^{club} singer.

2. In the eighties, many older women copied Madonna's style.

3. In 1987, Madonna started wearing rubber bracelets and changed her hair color.

4. Madonna dyed her hair for her role in *Evita*.

5. She adopted a mother image after her second child was born.

6. These days, fame and money are more important than her family.

2 What's "in"?

Writing

A Read the article. Replace each underlined adjective and expression with a similar one in the box.

| fashionable "in" in style "out" out of style popular the "in" thing ✓trendy |

Plan your new look!

You're ready to buy new clothes. But wait! Go shopping in your own closet first. Find colors that are ~~"in"~~ trendy this season, and see if they match with clothes you already have. Look at the colorful clothes people are wearing. Black will always be <u>fashionable</u>, but it's no longer the only choice. Add some tops in strong colors, since they are <u>the "in" thing</u> this year.

Casual dress is slowly going <u>out of style</u> –

sportswear is not as <u>popular</u> as it was some time ago. Your best bet is to buy classics that are going to be <u>in style</u> for a longer time. As for jeans, look for the <u>trendy</u> styles arriving in stores soon. Tight jeans will soon be <u>"out,"</u> so think carefully before buying.

Remember, you need to try on a lot of different styles to get a look that is right for you. Don't forget to have fun!

B Write a short article about new fashion trends using the expressions in part A.

Unit 11 Progress chart

Mark the boxes below to rate your progress. ✓ = I know how to . . . ? = I need to review how to . . .	To review, go back to these pages in the Student's Book.
Grammar ☐ use *have* and *have got* to describe people ☐ use phrases with verb + *-ing* and prepositions to identify people	108 and 109 111
Vocabulary ☐ name at least 14 expressions and adjectives to describe people	110 and 111
Conversation strategies ☐ show that I'm trying to remember a word ☐ use *You mean . . .* to help someone remember something	112 and 113 113
Writing ☐ use expressions to describe trends	115

Unit 12 Looking ahead

What's next?

1 Things that go together

Complete the phrases with the words in the box.

a baby	busy		for a new job	from college	some time off
✓abroad	for a master's degree		for a promotion	rich and famous	to another city

1. travel ___abroad___
2. have _____
3. become _____
4. take _____
5. keep _____

6. graduate _____
7. look _____
8. move _____
9. study _____
10. ask _____

2 We might move!

Grammar Read Rachel's e-mail. How sure is she that these things will happen? Circle the best future expressions to complete the sentences.

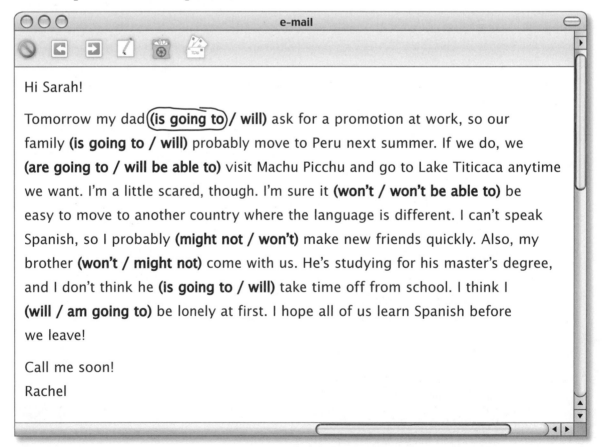

Hi Sarah!

Tomorrow my dad (**is going to** / **will**) ask for a promotion at work, so our family (**is going to** / **will**) probably move to Peru next summer. If we do, we (**are going to** / **will be able to**) visit Machu Picchu and go to Lake Titicaca anytime we want. I'm a little scared, though. I'm sure it (**won't** / **won't be able to**) be easy to move to another country where the language is different. I can't speak Spanish, so I probably (**might not** / **won't**) make new friends quickly. Also, my brother (**won't** / **might not**) come with us. He's studying for his master's degree, and I don't think he (**is going to** / **will**) take time off from school. I think I (**will** / **am going to**) be lonely at first. I hope all of us learn Spanish before we leave!

Call me soon!
Rachel

3 Planning ahead

Unscramble the questions. Then look at the pictures, and answer the questions.

MASTER'S DEGREE

1. she / going / look for a job / to / after graduation / Is ?

    Is she going to look for a job after graduation?

    No, she's going to study for a master's degree.

2. he / What / going / next summer / is / do / to ?

    _____

    _____

3. California / they / think / to / you / move / will / Do ?

    _____

    _____

4. is / What / goal / a year from now / her ?

    _____

    _____

5. think / he / be an English teacher / Does / he'll / after graduation ?

    _____

    _____

6. later this year / they / travel abroad / Will ?

    _____

    _____

91

1 *What do they do?*

 Write the names of the jobs under the pictures.

1. _____assistant_____

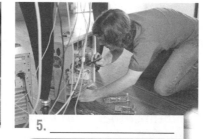

2. _____

3. _____

4. _____

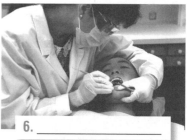

5. _____

6. _____

7. _____

8. _____

9. _____

10. _____

11. _____

12. _____

13. _____

14. _____

15. _____

16. _____

17. _____

18. _____

2 *What are your plans?*

Grammar Complete the conversations with the correct form of the verbs.

1. *Emily* How's your job going?

   Beth All right, I guess. It's just not very interesting. That's why I **'m taking** night
   ('m taking / 'll take)

   classes. After I _____ my degree next year, I _____ for a promotion.
   (get / 'll get)   (probably may ask / 'll probably ask)

   Emily When you _____ a promotion, will you earn more money?
   (get / won't get)

   Beth Sure. But I _____ any definite plans before I _____ my degree.
   (might not make / won't make)   (have / will have)

   Emily Night school sounds like hard work.

   Beth Yeah, it is, I guess. But next year at this time, I hope I _____ a manager.
   ('m going to be / 'll be)

   When I _____ a manager, I can relax.
   ('m / will be)

2. *Adam* What are you going to do after we _____ college?
   (finish / will finish)

   Neil I'm not sure. I _____ go to graduate school. How about you?
   (will / may)

   Adam Before I _____ any decisions, I think I _____ to my parents and ask
   (make / will make)   ('m going to talk / 'll talk)

   them for advice. If they _____ help me, I'll start my own business.
   (can / will be able to)

   Neil Sounds good. When your business _____ successful, will you give me a job
   (is / will be)

   after I _____ ?
   (graduate / will graduate)

   Adam Sure. If you _____ nicely.
   (ask / will ask)

3 *About you*

Grammar and vocabulary Complete the sentences with true information using *after*, *before*, *if*, or *when*.

1. I'm sure my family will be really happy ___if I get a master's degree_____ .

2. I may study _____ .

3. I hope I'll be able to _____ .

4. I might not get to _____ .

5. I guess I won't _____ .

6. I'll probably earn a lot of money _____ .

7. I'll be disappointed _____ .

1 Promises, promises

A Complete the conversations with the responses in the box.

✓I'll make the salad.	If you want, I'll call and remind you.
I won't forget.	I'll wake up on my own.
I won't be late.	I'll call you at 5:30, just in case.
I won't oversleep.	I'll let you borrow one of them.

1. *Liam* Hey, Elaine! We're having a class dinner this Saturday. Can you bring something?

    Elaine Sure. <u>I'll make the salad.</u>

    Liam Great! But don't forget the dressing like last time.

    Elaine _____ At least, I hope not.

    Liam _____

    Elaine Yeah, that might be good. Thanks.

2. *Jerry* Remember to set your alarm clock tonight. We're leaving at 6:00.

    Kevin Uh, I don't have an alarm, but it's all right. _____ I promise.

    Jerry I don't know. You might oversleep.

    Kevin Don't worry. _____

    Jerry You know, I have two alarm clocks. _____

    Kevin It's OK. _____ Really.

    Jerry _____

    Kevin Maybe I should just stay at your place tonight. That way you won't worry!

B Make an offer or promise using the words given.

1. *A* Will you remember to call the plumber this afternoon?

    B Yes. <u>I won't forget.</u>   (not forget)

2. *A* Oh, no! I forgot my cell phone. I have to call my brother for a ride home.

    B Don't worry. _____ (drive)

3. *A* I'm so hungry, and I left my lunch at home.

    B That's OK. _____ (money)

4. *A* I don't know what kind of computer to buy.

    B If you want, _____ (help).

5. *A* Who's going to take care of the children while I go grocery shopping?

    B _____ (do), but I have to leave by 4:00.

6. *A* I don't want to ride with you because you're never on time!

    B Don't worry. _____ (not be late)

2 A surprise party

Conversation strategies

Complete the conversation with the responses in the box.

> OK. I can take them to the post office on my way to work.
> All right. I'll make a chocolate one.
> OK, I guess. But how can you be tired? You didn't *do* anything.
> Um . . . all right. I'll pick her up on my way home. Anything else?
> ✓OK, no problem. I have plenty of space.
> All right. I know the perfect thing to buy!

Nicole Can we have Lynn's surprise party at your place? Mine's too small.

Tara   _OK, no problem. I have plenty of space._

Nicole And I'm a terrible baker. Could you make the cake?

Tara   _____

Nicole Could you also mail the invitations for me?

Tara   _____

Nicole And while you're doing that, would you mind getting Lynn a gift?

Tara   _____

Nicole Oh, and can you bring Lynn to the party that night?

Tara   _____

Nicole Yeah, just one more thing. I need a nap. Can you wake me up in an hour?

Tara   _____

3 A busy weekend

Conversation strategies

Respond to the requests. Then make an offer using your own ideas.

1. Could you make your special chicken recipe for us?   _All right. I'll make a salad, too._

2. Can you help me pick out some music?   _____

3. Could you pick me up on Saturday morning?   _____

4. Can you help me with my homework?   _____

5. Could you help me pack my stuff?   _____

1 *Travel planning*

Reading **A** Read the article. Then circle the best title.

Travel Now

Everyone's a travel agent!

THE FUTURE OF E-TICKETS

Do·it·yourself t o u r s

Frequent-flyer miles, bonus points, e-tickets, flexible-date searches – this isn't your grandmother's travel agency! The travel industry is changing, and as more people go online to make their own reservations, there will be less demand for traditional travel agents.

These trends are being encouraged by the major airlines and hotels, which offer discounts and specials to people who make their arrangements on the companies' Web sites. This saves the companies a lot of money because they don't have to hire as much staff.

Customer loyalty programs, such as frequent-flyer programs, have grown tremendously in recent years. People who use the same airline every time they travel are rewarded with points or miles, which they can exchange for free tickets. If customers buy e-tickets online, they are awarded bonus points.

However, more than 60% of online shoppers still make their final purchase through a travel agent over the phone. These people are generally more comfortable purchasing an actual paper ticket from a real person. But most experts agree that as more people get used to the do-it-yourself method, the way we approach travel could change in a variety of ways.

First, flexible-date searches, available on many airline sites, allow travelers to choose their dates according to cost. This could lead to more last-minute travel, as people with flexible schedules are able to save money. Second, people will be able to design their own tours and make their itineraries available to other travelers who might be interested in joining.

Next, since Web sites are cheap to run, more individuals will be able to start their own specialized online "agency." Finally, with all the options available online, there will be better-informed travelers – and probably more of them.

Although the number of traditional travel agents is decreasing, some people will always want to sit down with a real person and plan their trips. Many experts believe that just like online banking and shopping, the future of travel is in giving customers more choices, both online and off. And, like banking and shopping, online travel is making the world smaller – and a whole lot cheaper!

B Read the article again. Name four ways that the Internet will affect travel planning.

1. _____

2. _____

3. _____

4. _____

2 Life in the future

A Read the paragraph. Add *First, Second, Next,* and *Finally* to the paragraph to list the examples.

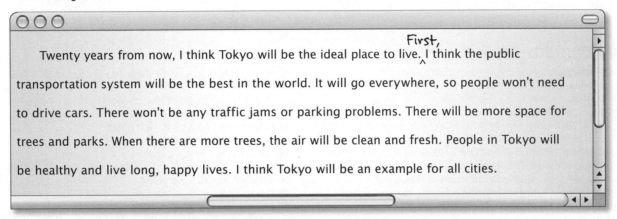

> First,
> Twenty years from now, I think Tokyo will be the ideal place to live. I think the public
> transportation system will be the best in the world. It will go everywhere, so people won't need
> to drive cars. There won't be any traffic jams or parking problems. There will be more space for
> trees and parks. When there are more trees, the air will be clean and fresh. People in Tokyo will
> be healthy and live long, happy lives. I think Tokyo will be an example for all cities.

B Write a short article about one of these topics. Use *First, Second, Next,* and *Finally* to list examples within the article.

- The ideal city of the future
- Health in the future
- Everyday life in the future
- The environment in the future

Unit 12 Progress chart

Mark the boxes below to rate your progress. ✓ = I know how to . . . ? = I need to review how to . . .	To review, go back to these pages in the Student's Book.
Grammar	
☐ use *will*, *may*, and *might* to talk about the future	118 and 119
☐ use the present continuous and *going to* for the future	118 and 119
☐ use the simple present in clauses with *if, when, after,* and *before* to refer to the future	121
Vocabulary	
☐ name at least 8 new expressions for work, study, or life plans	118 and 119
☐ name at least 15 different occupations	120 and 121
Conversation strategies	
☐ use *will* to make offers and promises	122 and 123
☐ use *All right* and *OK* to agree to do something	123
Writing	
☐ use *First, Second, Next,* and *Finally* to list ideas	125

Illustration credits

Kenneth Batelman: 42, 44
Dominic Bugatto: 14, 34, 82, 83
Daniel Chen: 6, 94
Matt Collins: 40, 72
Chuck Gonzales: 19, 29, 67, 75

Violet Lemay: 16, 78
Frank Montagna: 10, 22, 30, 58, 59, 69
Marilena Perilli: 5, 66, 70, 85
Greg White: 20, 47, 62, 63, 91
Terry Wong: 2, 3, 28, 55, 61

Photography credits

4 (*clockwise from top left*) ©Creatas; ©Index Stock; ©Creatas; ©Yuri Kadobnov/AFP/Getty Images/Newscom; ©Pegaz/Alamy; ©Punchstock
11 ©Stuart Pearce/age fotostock
12 (*top row, left to right*) ©Henry Diltz/Corbis; ©AP/Wide World Photos; ©Brett Coomer/AP/Wide World Photos; ©Frank Micelotta/Getty Images; (*bottom row, left to right*) ©Jennifer Szymaszek/AP/Wide World Photos; ©Tim Mosenfelder/Corbis; ©Mark J. Terril/AP/Wide World Photos; ©Robert Cianflone/Getty Images
13 (*top*) ©Robert E. Klein/AP/Wide World Photos; (*both bottom photos*) ©Lionel Hahn/Abaca Press/Newscom
15 (*both photos*) ©Punchstock
18 (*top*) ©David Schmidt/Masterfile; (*bottom*) ©Getty Images
21 (*clockwise from top left*) ©Mary Kate Denny/PhotoEdit; ©Dana White/PhotoEdit; ©Punchstock; ©Jose Luis Pelaez Inc./Corbis
24 (*left*) ©Alamy; (*right*) ©Surgi Stock/Getty Images
25 ©Punchstock
26 (*clockwise from top left*) ©Roberto Pfeil/AP/Wide World Photos; ©Russ Einhorn/Newscom; ©Chris Weeks/AP/Wide World Photos; ©Enrico Liverani/AP/Wide World Photos; ©Rufus F. Folkks/Corbis; ©JoeTakano/OrionPress/INFGoff.com/Newscom
31 ©Keren Su/China Span/Alamy
35 ©Michael Newman/PhotoEdit
39 ©Michael Newman/PhotoEdit
46 (*both photos*) ©Getty Images
48 (*clockwise from top left*) ©Carolina Biological/Visuals Unlimited; ©Ross Barnett/Lonely Planet Images; ©Alessandro Gandolfi/Index Stock
50 ©Ralph Lee Hopkins/Lonely Planet Images
51 ©White Packert/Getty Images
53 (*left to right*) ©Ken Lewis/Alamy; ©Eric Sanford/Index Stock; ©Bavaria/Getty Images

54 (*top*) ©Greg Elms/Lonely Planet Images; (*bottom*) ©Michael Goldman/Masterfile
56 (*left*) ©Joseph Van Os/Getty Images; (*right*) ©Chinch Gryniewicz/Corbis
64 both photos courtesy of Poezenboot
68 (*both photos*) ©Punchstock
76 (*left*) ©Corbis; (*right*) ©Creatas
77 ©Corbis
80 ©Raoul Minsart/Masterfile
82 ©Getty Images
84 (*top to bottom*) ©Punchstock; ©Getty Images; ©Punchstock
86 (*top to bottom*) ©Joerg Sarbach/AP/Wide World Photos; ©Stuart Franklin/Getty Images; ©Reuters/Corbis; ©Vince Bucci/Getty Images/Newscom
87 (*Yao Ming*) ©EPA/Michael Reynolds/Newscom; (*Black Eyed Peas*) ©Ric Francis/AP/Wide World Photos; (*Johnny Depp*) ©Rune Hellestad/Corbis; (*Salma Hayek*) ©UPI/Newscom; (*Venus and Serena Williams*) ©Lawrence Lucier/Getty Images/Newscom; (*high heels*) ©istock; (*man with spiked hair*) ©Alamy; (*man with mustache*) ©Getty Images
88 (*left to right*) ©Pizzoli Alberto/Corbis Sygma; ©Warner Bros/Everett Collection; ©Buena Vista Pictures/Everett Collection; ©Martin Cleaver/AP/Wide World Photos; ©Corbis Sygma
92 (*first row, left to right*) ©Punchstock; ©Corbis; ©Tom Carter/PhotoEdit; (*second row, all images*) ©Getty Images; (*third row, left to right*) ©Punchstock; ©Jeff Greenberg/PhotoEdit; ©Getty Images; ©Getty Images; (*fourth row, left to right*) ©David Young-Wolff/PhotoEdit; ©Getty Images; ©Corbis; ©Michael Newman/PhotoEdit; (*fifth row, left to right*) ©Robin Nelson/PhotoEdit; ©Antonio Mo/Getty Images; ©David J. Sams/Getty Images; ©Creatas
96 ©Punchstock

Text credits

Every effort has been made to trace the owners of copyrighted material in this book. We would be grateful to hear from anyone who recognizes his or her copyrighted material and who is unacknowledged. We will be pleased to make the necessary corrections in future editions of the book.